T0145490

STINKIN'
THINKIN'

STINKIN'
THINKIN'

**37 Mental Mistakes, False Beliefs
and Superstitions That Can Ruin
Your Career and Your Life**

Dr. Gary S.
Goodman

MEDIA

MEDIA

Published 2018 by Gildan Media LLC
aka G&D Media
www.GandDmedia.com

FIRST EDITION 2018

Front Cover design by David Rheinhardt of Pyrographx

Interior design by Meghan Day Healey of Story Horse, LLC

Library of Congress Cataloging-in-Publication Data is available upon request

ISBN: 978-1-7225-0013-9

10   9   8   7   6   5   4   3   2   1

Contents

Preface

I owe a debt of gratitude to the great motivational speaker, Zig Ziglar.

Early in my career I picked up a well-used copy of his classic self-help book: *See You At The Top*.

Zig wrote with wit and passion. He was one of the world's best salesmen for the power of maintaining a positive mental attitude.

Zig also mentioned, but only with a brief reference, that we should avoid putting garbage into our minds, what he termed "stinkin' thinkin."

That phrase stuck with me.

He didn't elaborate on what the many forms of sub-optimal thinking are, how they keep us from pursuing good and positive outcomes, and how they limit our careers and our lives.

I suppose he left that to me, providing part of the motivation to produce this program.

They say you can't help others without helping yourself at the same time.

By straightening out your thinking I'm reminding myself of the many traps we can fall into and tricks we can play on ourselves. Altogether, there are 37 tips that I offer to help you to avoid the mental mistakes, false beliefs, and superstitions that can ruin one's career and even one's life

I'm not going to sour your attitude by pointing out errors without also providing alternatives. I describe faults, but I provide prescriptions, as well.

You'll find lots of "do's" to go along with the "don'ts."

I think Zig would like that.

I look forward to clearing away the cobwebs, hobgoblins, and other mental distractions and miscalculations that have kept you from getting exactly what you want and what you deserve.

Please feel free to contact me with your questions, challenges, and success stories.

Best,

GARY

Dr. Gary S. Goodman

gary@negotiationschool.com

gary@customersatisfaction.com

gary@drgarygoodman.com

(818) 970-GARY (818) 970-4279.

Introduction

The quality of our thinking will largely determine the quality of our lives. If our thoughts are constructive, useful, clear, and unencumbered, we'll reach the gold standard of living well: We'll be happy.

On the other hand, if our thoughts are destructive, clouded, and barnacled we suffer. We usher into our careers and our personal lives nothing short of misery.

Beyond personal dissatisfaction we pay a huge price for allowing our thoughts to fail.

Bad thoughts cripple our careers. For instance, a tacit idea that we may have learned at home or picked up at school that "Corporations are inherently evil" can make us paranoid, setting-up in us a pattern of dissatisfaction whenever we interact with them.

My Dad felt this way about corporations. In his day he saw the rise of the Fortune-1000, the transnational organization, and the homogenization of much of American life. The factory model of production seemed to intrude into almost every aspect of living.

Suburbs were built with cookie cutter designs, each tract home identical to the next. Management strove to become scientific. Time-and-motion studies rooted out inefficiencies in manufacturing, and the same auditor's attitude started to hold accountable the service sector of the economy discouraging its wasteful ways.

Increasingly faceless firms replaced mom & pop businesses. The personal gave way to the impersonal.

Dad knew it was inevitable having to interact with behemoths, whether they were supermarket chains, hotels, health plans, and other providers of goods and services.

But he also worked for large companies, and he did so well with them that he was tapped to rise in the ranks. He almost always declined.

When they wanted to make him a sales manager, he wanted to stay in place as the top salesperson, instead.

I suppose he could have earned multiples of what he took home if he had answered the call. But whenever he got really comfortable at a big company, he found a way to generate a misunderstanding, have a spat, and leave in a huff.

This temperament brought its satisfactions. Periodically, he could expiate his hostilities, speak his mind, and feel autonomous.

It also gave him some downtime during which he could get off the merry-go-round and relax. He could spend more time at my Little League games and not have to travel around the country at a moment's notice.

He could say "NO!" when he wanted to, and he invoked this power often, I'm sure to at least his temporary delight.

But I don't believe he ever critically examined the basic premise that he carried around and shared with me, that corporations are rotten, and anti-humanistic.

Had he been more analytical about his thinking he would have empowered himself to make different choices. He could have just as easily have concentrated on the cornucopia of advantages big companies and complex organizations provide.

Scale economies in production enabled by conformity to certain processes created immense wealth. The standard of living around the world rose so quickly that millions of people were elevated from abject poverty into a growing middle class of income earners.

Public health and building standards made life safer and saved millions of lives while reducing disease, disasters, and suffering. "Bigness" could crush, but it could also create and uplift.

What you'll see in this program and what you can track in your life is the penalty that our prejudices provoke. At the same time, you'll appreciate the necessity and superior contribution made by intellectual humility.

By identifying the major assumptions we make about our careers and about organizations and other people we can ask ourselves this perspective-correcting question:

"And what if I'm wrong?"

Philosopher Bertrand Russell said it was this simple question that prevented him from flinging himself into causes that could have cost him his life.

A major theme of this program is that we cannot allow ourselves to engage in destructive and unproductive mental habits. Not in a world of competition, and in an increasingly unregulated, free-market world where our jobs, our incomes, and our security depend on effective mental processes.

Intellectually disabling ourselves in any way, by our own thinking, which is our habit and our everyday default setting, simply cannot be tolerated any more.

You've heard the adage, "If you can keep your head when everyone else is losing theirs."

This quote if from Rudyard Kipling;'s inspiring poem, "If," and it is worth reciting in full here as a benediction for our time together:

If you can keep your head when all about you
　　Are losing theirs and blaming it on you,
If you can trust yourself when all men doubt you,
　　But make allowance for their doubting too;
If you can wait and not be tired by waiting,
　　Or being lied about, don't deal in lies,
Or being hated, don't give way to hating,
　　And yet don't look too good, nor talk too wise:

If you can dream—and not make dreams your master;
　　If you can think—and not make thoughts your aim;
If you can meet with Triumph and Disaster
　　And treat those two impostors just the same;
If you can bear to hear the truth you've spoken
　　Twisted by knaves to make a trap for fools,

Or watch the things you gave your life to, broken,
  And stoop and build 'em up with worn-out tools:

If you can make one heap of all your winnings
  And risk it on one turn of pitch-and-toss,
And lose, and start again at your beginnings
  And never breathe a word about your loss;
If you can force your heart and nerve and sinew
  To serve your turn long after they are gone,
And so hold on when there is nothing in you
  Except the Will which says to them: 'Hold on!'

If you can talk with crowds and keep your virtue,
  Or walk with Kings—nor lose the common touch,
If neither foes nor loving friends can hurt you,
  If all men count with you, but none too much;
If you can fill the unforgiving minute
  With sixty seconds' worth of distance run,
Yours is the Earth and everything that's in it,
  And—which is more—you'll be a Man, my son!

Our program concentrates on weaknesses, poor mental habits and the kinds of thoughts that we need to examine critically and systematically to reduce or eliminate.

By the same token it lights the path to having better ideas and to charting a course of greater effectiveness in our lives and in our society.

There is a key assumption I bring to the task and I share, openly:

We are, or at least we can be the captains of our thoughts, and to a degree the marshals of our emotions.

The role of reasoned reflection can be greater in our lives than the role of raw reflexes.

This isn't to say bad or unfortunate things won't occur. They can, they do, and they will.

But as the ancient philosopher Epictetus said:

"It's not what happens to you but how you react that matters."

Let's make that reaction a thinking one, one that enables us to optimize our outcomes and our happiness.

Specifically, in the material to come, we'll examine many of the common thinking traps that we fall into. You'll learn to detect and then to self-correct when you are about to lead yourself astray.

You'll also spot the errors in thinking that those around you are making. You'll become less susceptible to the suasion of demagogues, con men and women, and those that want to take advantage of you.

In a very real sense, this is the most ambitious project that I've ever undertaken.

I'm excited about the prospects. If I can help you to improve your thinking this can translate into a world of advantages and benefits not only for you but also for everyone that is touched by your improved capabilities.

Welcome to this adventure. I hope you enjoy it as much as I do!

1

Should You Ask The Barber
if You Need a Haircut?

A few years ago a Southern California publishing company contacted me about doing some sales training.

This ended up being one of the most bizarre requests I ever fielded.

They told me their salespeople were already well trained, but they were hiring me to simply have a more credible outsider "Tell them the same things we've been telling them."

Coming from me, a best-selling author and accomplished presenter they felt the content would have a greater impact. Consequently, the troops would march the way they needed to march, which apparently they weren't doing based on what headquarters was teaching them.

This may seem like a slam-dunk, right? Don't break any new ground, just cover the ages-old verities and I'm home free.

I didn't see it that way.

I knew the techniques I taught, inside and out. I was expert in their use. But I had no way of knowing what the company had told its people. It would take a long time to find out.

And even if I did, what if what they were teaching was WRONG? There was a strong possibility of this.

In fact, my guess is that the troops weren't marching in a straight line because if they followed directions they'd stomp straight off a professional cliff getting fewer sales than what were getting at present.

Quite possibly, the marching orders were hopelessly flawed, and the company's established order didn't want to admit this and correct their errors.

Why would I rubber stamp directives I was unaware of?

Coming to me was like asking a barber if you need a haircut. Only the most unusual groomer will say no.

But that same barber will be flummoxed if you say, "Give me a haircut but leave every hair exactly the way it is."

Lurking beneath the surface is a sort of professional jealousy. The trainers that were bringing me in didn't want to be upstaged. But somehow they felt they had to bring me in, anyway.

I've seen something similar at work in people that seek out the help of attorneys. Some clients feel deficient that they have to get professional help, that they don't know enough to take matters into their own hands.

But instead of stating their problems and allowing the professionals to apply their knowledge and do their duty, some clients cannot resist competing with their attorneys. They invent their own outlandish theories of law and expect their counsel to pursue them.

"You just have a license but I have all the ideas" is what they seem to be saying.

The same sort of behavior troubles physicians. People complain about certain symptoms and then refuse to expose the area in question to eyes of the doctor.

We make a huge mental mistake when we pay people to tell us what we already know.

If you ask a barber if you need a haircut, be prepared to get one, not to cut your own while he watches and grimaces.

2

Beware of Correlations, Coincidences, Superstitions, & Random Strings of Things

Did you know that the murder rate seems to go up at the same time ice cream sales spike?

Males with a bigger middle finger to ring finger ratio seem to outscore others on the math portion of SAT tests. You didn't know that, did you?

These are correlations, events or phenomena that seem to be related.

Because our minds actively seek out patterns, we are always keen on connecting the dots and seeing meaningful relationships where there may not be any.

Sometimes, we mistake coincidence with correlation. You were just thinking of someone out of the blue, and then you run into her at the grocery store.

That's interesting, but it doesn't prove that thinking about people causes you to see them in short order.

Who would need phones or communication if this were the case?

I know people that believe there are certain good digits and bad digits on license plates. If they see 777 or even better, 7777 on a plate, this bodes well for the immediate future.

On the other hand, if they see 666 or 6666, then trouble lies ahead.

What are they apt to do if licenses go one way or another? Crawl back into bed? Boldly ask the boss for a raise?

You can see that these events are not connected, but we want them to be, especially if the signs seem positive.

People also read into events significance based on the frequency of good or bad things happening. Finding a piece of jewelry on the sidewalk or a hundred dollar bill certainly seems fortunate.

On the same day, if you are an instant winner in the supermarket's contest and you walk away with a free turkey, this means you're on a roll.

Go ahead and invest your life's savings in lottery tickets because today is your lucky day!

Not a good idea, because we are being "fooled by randomness."

It isn't good luck that we're benefitting from but one of those strings of things that will occur, statistically, every now and then.

My mother drove a car for forty years without incident and then in a single day she was ticketed for two moving violations.

Had her skills diminished so much, overnight? Was she really a suddenly awful driver that should be removed from traffic?

Frankly, she had her doubts after that day. Her self-image as a fantastic driver took not just one hit but two hits, in rapid succession and she started to read into those events an ominous message.

"Maybe I'm losing it, fast!"

More likely, was the fact that she made two detectible boo-boos that two different cops witnessed and wrote up.

We have expressions for chains of events and correlations.

"When you're hot you're hot, and when you're not, you're not" is one of them.

"Don't press your luck" is another one.

Being "accident-prone" is how some folks are labeled and how others define themselves.

Believing this can become a self-fulfilling prophecy. If we fail to be cautious and to heed proper safety warnings, then we'll have mishaps and perhaps more than others have.

If we feel destined to experience these pratfalls, what motivation do we have to take extra precautions if we think we're doomed, anyway?

Ever walk under a ladder? Ever wonder where that superstition comes from?

Somebody probably did that and something fell on his head or the ladder collapsed. But a mistake was made in retelling the tale.

It was said that walking under the ladder CAUSED the bad outcome.

All things that precede others are not causes. It is a mistake to think they are.

You wear a hat inside the house and the roof starts to leak. Did one cause the other?

Superstitions would have us believe that.

The problem with all of these mental mistakes is that they waste our time and dissipate our focus. They also send a message that outside forces are mainly responsible for our outcomes instead of self-directed action.

Thus they promote passivity instead of positive activity.

Much like medical quackery, where the advice given isn't harmful per se, superstitions and other errors in thought prevent us from seeking other "cures" that we might discover and put to good use but-for the fact that we're preoccupied with drivel.

In other words stinking thinking pushes out better, more productive thinking, and this is a fact that we need to acknowledge and correct.

3

Letting The Dead Hand
of the Past Strangle New Ideas

One of the ways we let stinking thinking ruin our lives and especially our careers is by letting tradition strangle new ideas and innovation.

"We've always done it this way" is used as a justification to smother change in its infancy.

This is not to say all change is good. Sometimes it isn't. Famously, Coke changed the formula for its soda without telling consumers. They rebelled, quite loudly, and sales plummeted.

Quickly, that giant and otherwise hugely successful company recanted and reissued "Classic Coke," using the tried-and-true formula.

Companies are really on the horns of a dilemma when it comes to innovation. They have an obvious and justified attachment to what made them prosper. At the same time, they need to relentlessly expand their markets and their product lines to grow their profits and to make shareholders happy.

This makes the "abandonment decision" as Peter F. Drucker called it, very difficult to make.

Exactly when can a company, or an individual evaluating the progress of her career, know it's time to let go and to move on to something new?

Certainly, when profits lag, when competitors enter the market with lower prices, higher quality, better service or some other competitive advantage, it is time to revalue one's exposure.

The risk isn't doing something new. It is continuing to stay with the old.

The Blockbuster video chain was in the business of renting and selling movies at a handsome profit. Redbox, a start-up with far lower costs entered the picture, renting and receiving back into inventory videos at a dollar each.

Blockbuster was charging about $4.50 and it was harder to do business with.

Clearly, something had to give. Blockbuster went bankrupt and closed most of its stores. Then it got into the kiosk business, side by side with Redbox.

But Blockbuster tried to charge up to $4 for a video, still. It failed, miserably. Redbox survives, with slightly higher prices, but it has also lost market share to streaming services such as Netflix, Hulu, and Amazon.

There are risks you cannot afford to take. And there are risks you cannot, NOT afford to take.

You can just imagine the conversation inside of Blockbuster as it moved into kiosk rentals.

"We've always gotten $4 and up for a rental!"

"Yeah, but Redbox is down at $1."

"They're crazy."

The dead hand of the past wanted $4 a rental.

When should you retool your career or move on to a different kind of opportunity?

Back in the day, there was such a functionary known as an Executive Secretary. Ray Kroc, the McDonalds chain founder had one. She stayed with Kroc for many years.

Along the way, he gave her stock options that she cashed in. This made her one of the richest executive secretaries on Earth.

Her loyalty and obvious capability were rewarded.

But staying with one company for decades these days is very unlikely, and not necessarily desirable.

In sales work there is an expression that selling is as easy as ABC. This stands for Always Be Closing.

There is an ABC to career success. Always Be Canvassing for a bigger and better opportunity.

You may be comfortable where you are, like the people, and tell yourself it's "family," but this is exactly when you should be looking for something better.

Don't allow yourself to become complacent.

It is equivalent to letting the dead hand of the past strangle your future.

4

Don't Sit On Your Best Ideas, Disseminate Them

Much of this project is dedicated to identifying and then reducing or altogether eliminating defective thoughts.

But what if you have a great idea, something that is definitely worth sharing, and possibly it's a breakthrough?

Of course that's wonderful and if you're like me the energy released by a great idea is like nuclear fission.

I was reading an article in the *New York Times*, entitled "Don't Just Solve a Problem, Go Tell the World." The article is counter-intuitive and thus, potentially quite valuable. The problem we face is in disseminating great ideas, not in having them. Let me quote directly from the writer, Tina Rosenberg:

> *"Have you thought of a clever product to mitigate climate change? Did you invent an ingenious gadget to light African villages at night? Have you come up with a new kind of school, or new ideas for lowering the rate of urban shootings?*

"Thanks, but we have lots of those," says Rosenberg.

"Whatever problem possesses you, we already have plenty of ways to solve it.

"Many have been rigorously tested and have a lot of evidence behind them—and yet they're sitting on a shelf.

"So don't invent something new. If you want to make a contribution, choose one of those ideas—and spread it.

"Spreading an idea can mean two different things. One is to take something that's working in one place and introduce it somewhere else. If you want to reduce infant mortality in Cleveland, why not try what's working in Baltimore?

"Well, you might not know about what's working because there's no quick system for finding it.

"Even when a few people do search out the answer, innovative ideas don't spread by themselves. To become well known, they require effort from their originators. For example, a Bogotá, Colombia, maternity hospital invented Kangaroo Care—a method of keeping premature babies warm by strapping them 24/7 to Mom's chest. It saved a lot of lives in Bogotá. But what allowed it to save lives around the world was a campaign to spread it to other countries."

Ms. Rosenberg makes a compelling point. Although I'm sure she really doesn't want to put a damper on having good ideas, the distribution of breakthroughs is exceedingly challenging.

In my doctoral program we studied the "Communication of Innovations. " There was an assigned book by Rogers and Shoemaker bearing that very title.

It seems many of the most significant improvements in living standards, particularly in the developing world, follow a distinctive sequence.

First, opinion leaders must try the innovation. If they like it, and they endorse it, the majority of potential users begin to embrace it. Finally, late adopters and then laggards get with the program and start to use whatever it is.

Ms. Rosenberg's point is that you can assist at any one of these junctures. You can identify a potential champion of a concept, or you can assist in taking an existing endorsement and publicizing it.

The point here is that you may very well build a better mousetrap but the world will find a way to avoid your doorstep and remain ignorant about it.

Unless, that is, you make your breakthrough known.

One of the greatest innovations in medicine was the reduction of post-operatives deaths resulting from operating room infections. According to Peter F. Drucker, who studied the diagnostic capabilities of physicians, the simple yet effective practice of having surgeons wash their hands before procedures prevented countless deaths, once it was known there was a connection between hand-washing and infections.

In those days of slow and spotty communications, it took some time to get the word out.

The point here is that sitting on a good idea is a very bad idea.

I devised a special conversational sequence for improving the cost effectiveness of customer service conversations. Service reps didn't have a good way to end conversations, so they would ramble on. This prevented reps from assisting others that were waiting in the cue.

Plus, customers and clients really appreciated more succinct conversations, because their time was being saved, as well.

I brought my technique to some major companies that saved millions of hours of talk-time and thus many millions of dollars.

But I realized that if my idea was to gain any widespread impact, I had to write a book, which I did do.

To this day, I hear fragments of my conversational path being used on me from various sources, most of which I didn't directly train.

That's because my innovation was communicated.

Don't sit on yours. If you do, your best thinking will become stinking thinking from disuse.

5

You Are Not Powerless

Perhaps the worst form of stinking thinking is to underestimate your personal power.

I like to summon to mind the movie, "The Martian," starring Matt Damon.

He was knocked unconscious and impaled by a super-propelled metallic pole. A huge windstorm required the rest of the crew to take off and leave the planet, and Damon's character was marooned.

If ever there was a fast start to a movie, this is it. The balance of the tale is about Damon's survival on that inhospitable orb.

Everything seems to conspire against him. His oxygen and food are dissipating. He has no way to communicate with mission control. Even if they could launch a rescue mission, it would take too long to reach him.

Dauntless, Damon starts tackling these obstacles, one by one. I love this film because it shows the resilience of the human spirit, our practically infinite ability to create and to improvise, and the truly extraordinary power we can exert over our environments and ourselves.

There are several lessons to be drawn from the movie about our personal power. For one thing, when we seem to have no options, we still have options. We simply haven't generated them, yet.

Using his knowledge of science, Damon manufactured his own oxygen. He grew his own food.

He rigged an abandoned Mars probe so it could signal he was alive, and actually transmit and receive text messages.

This is one of the movies that you leave, as I did in the late afternoon, and I was thrilled to feel the wind in my face and the sun in my eyes. Just being in my own element was gratifying after witnessing what he went through.

We forget how many options we have. And it is all too easy to succumb to excuses and to stereotypes.

Stephen Hawking was arguably the smartest scientist in the world. A debilitating and degenerative disease robbed him of much of the physical functionality you and I take for granted.

Still, he produced astonishing insights into the origins and possible outcomes of the universe. When he was interviewed he mentioned that he felt very lucky and life had exceeded his expectations.

He made the most of what he had, and that adds up to huge contributions to science and humanity.

When I was reading about the philosophy of science, I came across a great quote:

"There is nothing as practical as a good theory."

The idea is that if we develop a good theory it can lead us to understand and then to master a constellation of related things. Theory unifies our understanding, and simplifies it in ways that "get down to business," to borrow from the slogan of a famous science-based enterprise.

Sometimes a theory is just a hunch, a working hypothesis, a postulate, and we go on from there, pretending that it explains things correctly.

For instance, I'm going to postulate that there is no such thing as a "hopeless" situation. We always have choices that can be made, even if we think they are less than optimal or even less than desirable.

Let me give you an example. Millions of people are turning 65 years of age each and every day. This is one of the most rapidly increasing age cohorts on the planet.

In America, age 65 has borne certain connotations. Because it is one of the ages most associated with drawing Social Security compensation and Medicare coverage, 65 is the primary age equated with "retirement."

If you are approaching 65 or you have reached it, societal norms, expressed to you over and again through advertising and other ways, you are expected to dramatically downshift your professional activities.

You are also expected to be far less employable than you were 10, 15, 20, and 25 years before. Don't bother seeking work because it probably isn't there for you; this is the notion that is widely propagated.

Or if you find it, you'll be a "Greeter" at the mouth of a department store, or another type of limited contributor.

What if Social Security isn't enough for you to live on? What can you do to make ends meet?

Not a whole lot, is the current conception.

True for some, this certainly isn't true for all.

As I've written in my book and said in my audio book, *The Forty Plus Entrepreneur,* there is the option to start your own business at age 40, 50, 60, and beyond.

In fact, the average age of business-starters is over 35, and many famous entrepreners set forth on their own past 50, including Ray Kroc of McDonalds, and Colonel Harlan Sanders of Kentucky Fried Chicken. It was Sanders' paltry Social Security check that got him to start his famous poultry business.

Age is also becoming something beyond the physical and chronological. Given greater awareness of health and diet, people are living longer than ever before.

Being in one's 70's, while not the pluck of youth, is definitely not the old age it was perceived as being only a few decades ago.

Living past 100, in relatively good health, is becoming so commonplace as to not be all that exceptional.

The idea that I started with, that at age 65 you need to start trimming back your activities or retire, is nonsense. It isn't a fact of life, as it has been long regarded.

People are violating this expectation all the time.

Age is a mere opinion about life. It is a perception, and like all perceptions it is subject to modification.

Many of my best teachers were well over age 65 when I took their courses. Peter F. Drucker was in his middle 80's when I took my MBA classes with him and got to know him, personally.

He stayed active, lecturing, consulting, and teaching into his 90's.

Dr. Albert Ellis, famed psychologist who I mention elsewhere, was in his 70's when I studied with him. Donald C. Bryant was past 80 when I did some of my best intellectual work in my doctoral program.

They realized they had options to keep contributing, and that's exactly what they did, as I know, first hand.

Baseball's legendary quipster, Yogi Berra noted: "It ain't over 'til it's over."

And an even wiser soul added, "And it's never over."

That is, it isn't over unless you make that decision. Until that time, you have options, more than you know.

Even if you're stuck on Mars!

6

Overcoming Ambivalence

In one of the "Batman" movies, the comical villain Two-Face wisecracks that he is "of two minds" about something or other.

Two faces, two minds; get it?

Well, it is funny in context.

But generally, being of two minds about some topic or potential action or choice causes pain and it results in procrastination, a failure to act.

Ben Franklin, one of the wisest of America's Founding Fathers, suggested a simple procedure for making decisions. Make one list of advantages and at the right of that, list the disadvantages.

The longer list wins.

Pretty simple, isn't it?

But let's slow down. You might say I'm of two minds when it comes to using this technique. On the one hand, it is simple, quick, and straightforward.

Want a new computer? It will be faster, more functional, and probably easier to defend from nasty viruses.

Plus, it will be an aesthetic change of pace, probably with a nicer screen resolution and different color.

Of course, cost is the major negative, plus transferring your data, and then there's the question of what to do with the old one. Trash it? Destroy the hard drive? Give it away?

Maybe you don't need a new computer, after all.

There's more to every decision than meets the eye if we take the time to fashion a list of pros and cons. We could also factor in the unintended consequences.

Because a new computer will be faster this may mean we can download faster and view more movies in less time and multitask with more open applications. This means we may usher in distractions and actually get less work done with a newer device.

The downside of old Ben's prescription is we can jimmy the results so we have an equal number of pluses and minuses, more or less guaranteeing that we do nothing definitive.

Lists of advantages and disadvantages can be an excuse to perpetuate our ambivalence.

Let's deconstruct the word, ambivalence, and we can see the problem clearly.

It means being of two valences, and this means each of two options has an importance to us.

You'd like your child to learn to play the piano. It is a beautiful skill to have, and it is a treat for a lifetime. Plus it presents a social opportunity inasmuch as she can entertain friends.

But you'd also like your child to play an after school sport. She can be in the fresh air, benefit from the exercise, and also polish her social skills.

She doesn't have sufficient time to do both.

This is comparing apples and oranges, in many ways.

Piano and softball are two different skills, so how do you develop a basis of comparison that can help you to add valence or additional "charge" to one of the choices, ridding you of that uncomfortable ambivalence?

A way to do this is to ask: Which of the choices will remain after the other one is chosen. In other words, can I postpone one without jeopardizing it?

Piano should be started earlier, from a developmental standpoint. It is more of a discipline than a form of recreation, especially in the beginning.

You can always try out for a sport, and while those that begin sooner are more familiar with the rules, and they have greater experience with it, they may also be limited by their innate skill or physiognomy.

There are numerous major league baseball players that actually starred in a different sport such as football. Late in the game, so to speak, they switched over to baseball and actually became respected professionals.

Another aspect of eliminating an option is to ask: Can the benefits of this alternative be obtained another way?

Fresh air and exercise can be gained in many ways, not the least of which is by walking or running. In the middle of that piano lesson, or afterwards, the child can take a walk around the block with the teacher to discuss technique or musical selections to be learned.

The teacher-student interaction is also a social experience, though we don't consider it as such. You learn in the presence and under the guidance of someone else, whose direction you need to accept in order to become more competent.

The piano teacher is a coach just as that softball coach is a coach.

Are there bigger "life lessons" attached to one activity over another?

What is the long-range impact of dedicating oneself to the piano versus to a sport?

Disclosure: I was a baseball player and not a pianist. My kids are pianists.

I was the captain of many sports teams so I learned some leadership and team-building skills. These have helped me professionally as a manager and as an organization-building consultant.

But I believe learning piano probably would have inculcated discipline at a younger age. This, along with the requirement to continually practice on my own could have driven home the importance of working independently and taking responsibility.

Still, I was self-supporting and on my own at age 18, working my way through college, so I certainly became highly disciplined when I needed to.

Finally, when we're facing ambivalence, we need to ease-up on ourselves, realizing we cannot have all the facts in advance.

Aristotle pointed out that we live in a world of probabilities and not certainties. We may steer a child into an activity because it is a family tradition. Yet he or she may have no aptitude for it, whatsoever.

Take an experimental attitude. "We'll try the piano" is a much better stance to take than insisting that a child sign-up for a year of lessons.

I can tell you from having coached three major kids' sports, softball, soccer, and basketball that the child that performs the worst is also the unhappiest. And that kid makes the exercise much less fun for everyone else.

Feel little or no ego-investment in sticking to an activity that isn't a good fit. Move on as quickly to something that will be more gratifying.

Unless, that is, you main value is discipline. Then, sticking to anything will probably do.

The problem with ambivalence, being of two minds about something is that it is psychologically uncomfortable. It presents us with an "open issue" when our minds crave closure.

And because a subject is open we tend to fixate on that problem instead of feeling free to move on to something else. It wastes our time and we get less done.

Knowing our progress is slowing or at a standstill, we think less of ourselves and lose self-confidence. Without positive self-regard we are likely to become even less decisive and more ambivalent, with time.

How do we stop this habit? Do these four things:

1. Recognize the standoff between two options.

2. You can put your decision on a timer allowing yourself only 48 hours to choose one over the other.

3. You can diminish the value of both options and do nothing.

4. You can generate a third option that incorporates the pluses of the other two while diminishing their downsides. (Have your child join a marching band, getting exercise and musical training!)

Following this process will bring you a sense of relief and enable you to move on to other things.

7

Are You Paranoid or A Prophet?

According to a recent article in the *New York Times* George Orwell's dystopian future depicted in *1984* is at hand, more ominous and irrepressible than ever.

It is being brought to us and even to our households via the Internet-of-things, as it is called. Everyday objects and devices are becoming smarter and soon they will gather and transmit data about our habits, impulses, and perhaps even our thoughts.

Your refrigerator will constantly perform an inventory control function. Just as the bar code scans tell supermarkets when to automatically reorder peanut butter, your fridge will contribute to and update your shopping list.

It may also rat you out to your physician and to your insurance companies whose list of forbidden foods has made certain common substances verboten given your genotype and health history.

Your couch will collect and transmit information about your inactivity while also monitoring your respiration, heart rate, and blood pressure.

Our TV's are already telling tales about our viewing preferences, and these in turn are revealing much about our politics, mores, and tattle on our offbeat or suspicious preferences.

In certain parts of the world, say in London for example, it is practically impossible to walk down a city street without being on closed circuit television. With existing facial recognition software you can not only be spotted but also be tagged and tracked, step by step.

Smart phones giveaway our whereabouts with GPS precision where occasional CCTV blind spots occur. When we escape from city to suburbs or to the countryside, drones can surveil us from the skies.

We know our Internet browsing histories are available to not only service providers but also to Big Brother units of national intelligence services.

I was debating a fellow on CNBC television who had invented software that would track what we say in phone conversations. Based on that content advertisements would pop-up on our computer screens.

This was actually a business proposition. By permitting this intrusion we would receive free or subsidized phone service, for our troubles.

I slammed the idea. To me, forfeiting the privacy that I expect when I speak to anyone over the phone is a huge price to pay for something as trifling as a lower phone bill. In fact, at practically any price, being monitored like that, having my comments constantly scrutinized, classified, and judged is fraught with concerns.

The awareness of incessant monitoring is one thing. It is rational. But when concern becomes magnified, multiplied, and obsessive, it can metastasize into what we call paranoia.

Webster defines paranoia as:

1. a psychosis characterized by systematized delusions of persecution or grandeur usually without hallucinations
2. a tendency on the part of an individual or group toward excessive or irrational suspiciousness and distrustfulness of others

However, just because you smell a rat, sense something is awry, this doesn't mean you're suffering from stinking thinking.

As the joke puts it: "Just because you're paranoid this doesn't mean they *aren't* out to get you.

You could be extreme in your sensitivities and also be correct.

This can become a self-fulfilling prophesy, especially in a "surveillance society," which many believe we have already become.

For instance if you are hyper-concerned about being monitored, you might act in an aberrant manner. You could select a dozen different ways to drive to work, stopping frequently to see if any cars are tailing you.

You might purchase a huge supply of burner phones that purportedly allow you to make anonymous, hard-to-trace calls.

If you do enough of these things, it could seem to authorities that you have something to hide. Once they suspect this, they could very well do the exact things you've been in your paranoid state expecting them to do.

Joseph Stalin, the Russian head of state who reportedly was responsible for putting to death up to 30 million of his countrymen, believed "No man is innocent."

He knew if he dug deeply enough and widely enough he could find incriminating dirt on anyone. Thus, if he wrongly punished or exiled a person to Siberia for a crime the person did not commit Stalin could say with confidence the punishment was justified based on all of the undetected bad acts the person did commit.

Constitutional law scholars point to the "chilling effect" various measures have on our civil liberties. Specifically, if we feel being spied on is continuous and inescapable then we'll change our habits of communication and interpersonal association.

Fearing guilt-by-association we'll shy away from eccentric people, whether they are artists, professors, writers, politicians, philosophers, musicians, or simply next-door neighbors.

These odd types will self-censor their work products, sanitizing them so they become less and less offensive. The net effect of surveillance will be to put everyone into a fishbowl, from which there will be no practical escape, civil liberties experts say.

Science fiction author Ray Bradbury had an interesting take on his prophetic writing. He said:

"I don't try to predict the future. I try to prevent it."

He didn't prevent the proliferation of TV screens in every room of the house. He didn't prevent the incessant chirping of vapid communications between people using hand held devices and earplugs.

But he did accurately predict them.

The problem with paranoia is that it is a moving target; the goal posts are constantly changing.

The persons that saw in computers devices with the potential to rob individuals of their jobs and their livelihoods was delusional, measured by the power of those early machines several decades ago.

Computers have replaced millions of jobs during the last twenty years. That same paranoid individual was simply a visionary, slightly ahead of his time.

How many secretaries does it take to organize and to administer today's work in corporations? They've all but disappeared. Once, they did all of the typing and phone call taking and placement for executives.

They have been replaced by voice mail and by the expectation that everyone will do his or her own typing and email correspondence.

Robots have replaced auto factory workers but they are becoming so highly programmed and designed that they'll do complicated medical procedures in the near future.

Let's hark back to those definitions of paranoia that I offered earlier. What exactly, is the standard by which we determine whether someone is afflicted with "excessive or irrational suspiciousness and distrustfulness of others?"

It is hard to say. But today, we shouldn't be quite so trigger-happy as to impulsively label someone as being "paranoid," as we might have done in years past.

By contemporary standards, they may seem out of sync with the times, but they, like Bradbury, might be focused on preventing a future that the rest of us in our rational states, just cannot see.

Yet.

8

To All Lend Your Ear,
But To Few Thy Tongue

I've made a few dumb mental mistakes in my career and I'm at the point where I can admit them.

By doing so I hope to spare you the trouble of erring as I did.

I was invited to speak before a national meeting of a trade association in Las Vegas. This was a well-paid, major event for me, and I was looking forward to it.

Around that same time period I was cultivating a strategic relationship with a fellow that was an even more experienced, big-time speaker.

Our topics differed, so I believed that we were not competitors.

To establish my credibility I rattled off to him a list of successful speaking events that I did. He asked me what was up next on my schedule.

"I have a Las Vegas convention that I'm doing in April," I replied.

Who is this for?

I mentioned the group's name and he just said, "Oh," and our conversation continued.

The next thing I knew I was at the site of that convention speech. There was a speaker going on before me.

Who was it? It was a clone of the guy I was trying to befriend. This was the cheaper, plain-wrapped version of my contact.

What happened next blew me away.

The clone gave a talk that totally stole my thunder. It was on my exact speech topic, and he lifted material right from the pages of my books.

Worse, the audience liked him!

I delivered one of the least satisfying talks of my budding career.

I found out the fellow I was trying to partner with was a long-time speaker for the very same association and at the last minute he got a pal of his on the speaker selection committee to add the clone to the agenda, purposely positioning that dude's talk right before mine.

I kicked myself for trying to team up with a rattlesnake.

And I learned an important lesson. You can be way too open about your ideas and if you confide in the wrong types, you'll invite problems.

I've seen something similar in the publishing business. Proposing a book title to various editors, I've received some rejections. Then, one publisher will agree to do the book, I'll write it, and it will get published.

Suddenly, after mine appears, I'll see a competing volume with substantially the same title. I published *Six-*

Figure Consulting and seemingly a month or two later, *Million Dollar Consulting* came out.

If you had to select one or the other, which would you choose? The one with the bigger promise in the title, correct?

I published *Dr. Gary S. Goodman's 60 Second Salesperson.* Soon after that, I spotted *The One Minute Salesperson.*

There is an adage used often as a joke, "Great minds think alike." Also, just because I have an idea for a title doesn't mean I have an exclusive on that title.

Still, these coincidences are disappointing and deflating. I've seen enough of them to infer there is a tendency toward foul play.

One of Shakespeare's characters offers advice to his son before the boy ventures into the world, on his own. Essentially, papa advises:

"To All Lend Your Ear, But To Few Thy Tongue."

Meaning, keep your mouth shut, listen up, and you'll save yourself from a number of woes. You'll also learn much if you listen more than you speak.

We cannot know whom to trust, in advance.

I experienced a lot of success with my seminars, so much so that I needed to clone myself. I couldn't handle the increasing demand for my content, by myself.

I had worked with a very good trainer in a program we did for the U.S. Navy. He was well liked and seemed to be able to think on his feet.

I hired him to co-teach one of my programs, which he did with some success.

Before I realized it, he was offering his own version of my seminar on his own, without a license.

There is always a balancing act between silence and speaking. We have to weigh the merits of disclosing vital information or keeping it to ourselves.

Working my way through college, as I mentioned elsewhere, I was a salesperson and a sales manager for a large publishing company.

I did very well, and the thought occurred to me that there was a business opportunity staring us in the face, given how successful we were.

We could start a consulting business aimed at teaching the sales and marketing skills we were using to such great advantage, every day. I even mentioned this concept to my manager at the time.

"No, I don't think so," he said, dismissively.

It was apparent he had enough on his plate. He was earning a ton, lived well and drove a top of the line Mercedes.

I tucked away that thought.

I asked myself, what would it take for me to position myself as a credible consultant?

"A Ph.D. would do nicely," was the answer.

Eight years after I had that idea for a consulting practice I made my first call pitching a seminar to a university on that topic.

They agreed, I taught it, and I was on my way.

During that 8 year span I earned three degrees: the BA, MA, and Ph.D..

I also taught at the university level for four of those years.

When I returned to my alma mater to take one of my doctoral professors to lunch, he remarked glowingly about the top of the line Mercedes convertible I was driving.

"Where did all of this come from?" he asked about my astonishing success.

Neither he nor any other professor of mine had heard me speak about my idea for a consulting business. I never wrote a paper on the subject.

All of which was on purpose. I was secretive about my plans.

I intuited that I would be better off to mask my ultimate intentions. It was an advantage to teach and to become a capable speaker, and to have my doctoral degree in hand before starting a fledgling enterprise.

I was living the truth of that Shakespearean advice.

I kept my mouth shut and I thrived.

Sometimes we're so proud of our ideas that we can't help but share them with others.

But this can be a mistake. Often it is better to "Keep your own counsel," as Shakespeare put it.

9

Defining The Problem Incorrectly

The U.S. space program faced a problem. Astronauts didn't have a pen that could write inside a zero gravity capsule. NASA invested upwards of $1 million to devise a pen that could.

The Russians faced the same problem, but they solved it for less than a dollar.

They decided to use a pencil.

This story is emblematic of two styles of critical thinking and problem solving. America defined its quandary as a "pen" problem. "Fix the pen" became the marching order.

Others defined the issue as a "writing" challenge, so alternatives were more likely to be considered and adopted.

Parents make the same mistake when they uproot the family and move to a new neighborhood.

I can tell you from personal experience that it is never easy finding the "right school" for one's pewees.

You have to do your research. Look into the rankings.

Then you need to ask huge either-or questions: Public or private school; parochial or independent?

A lot is riding on these answers.

Let's say you choose to move to an area with schools that post great test scores and boast about wonderful college placements for graduates. What could be better, right?

But wait a second. You have to pay double or triple for your existing rent or mortgage to afford living quarters in that village.

How are you going to do it? If one of you stays at home now, that person might have to enter or return to the workforce. You'll have two incomes, you can pay the nut, but what if one mate loses his or her job?

And there will be child-care costs. You'll need to arrange trusted, but economically viable assistance.

A private school will cost a lot, as well. Plus, complicating matters is the fact that you probably can't write-off the tuition on your taxes. You'll be supporting that leafy institution with after-tax dollars.

Ouch!

You could stay where you are, in your currant locale, but you're paranoid about violence finding its way into schools and the prospect of surrounding your kids with disruptive influences.

Quite a conundrum, isn't it?

But in a very real way this is simply the NASA pen-hunt all over again. Remember, they defined the task as developing a PEN that could write in a zero-gravity environment where ink normally won't flow.

But rivals were more focused on the end-result of finding a suitable writing instrument. They focused on TAKING NOTES, which is the task that a writing instrument accomplishes.

In my narrative above I have treated the challenge as finding and affording a good school for one's child. The presumption has been that such as school would have to be located somewhere, and definitely where the family currently doesn't reside.

That's not the challenge. The challenge can be restated various ways. Here is one of them.

What kind of school can offer a cost-effective, fine education in an ultra-safe environment, free from distracting peer pressures and potential violence?

Let's skip to the answer: Home schooling!

For safety, there's no place like home.

In a family where one parent is already staying home with the children, or where a parent or guardian wants to do so, home schooling is ideal.

You don't have to move from one place to another because the school is coming to you and you're going to it, online. This is going to save you money.

I can tell you from personal experience that home school is a smashing success for my family. We live in what we consider to be an ideal place, on a channel with boats and beautiful vistas.

But the nearby schools, public and private, are simply average.

However, the county wide home school system is excellent, and the tuition is free, already paid through our taxes.

My kids are doing advanced work and there is plenty of time for piano, ice-skating, ballet, swimming and surfing.

How you state your challenge or your problem will inform the quality of answer you get.

Thinking improves by forming the issue in various ways.

Peter F. Drucker, my often quoted mentor and management guru was fond of asking top executives this question: What business are you really in?

Most heard this query and then they replied with the obvious.

At Time-Life Books my New York boss visited and asked me: "Gary, what business are we in?"

I sensed it was a trick question but I couldn't help answering it incorrectly, anyway.

"We're in the BOOK business, Gerry!"

"What if I told you we're in the name business, the list development business; would you believe me?"

He went on to say only 3% of the American public at the time read books. Our job was to expand that number, to make more of the 97% of non-readers, book lovers.

It was a very interesting and eye opening conversation!

If your focus is on being in the book business you'll compete against other publishers for the same, small audience. If you're in the new-name or list building business, you'll go after a much larger market.

Gillette is one of the most successful, old-line companies in the world. It is part of the Dow-30 industrial stock index. Billionaire Warren Buffett, perhaps the world's greatest stock inventor thinks s so much of Gillette that his holding company, Berkshire Hathaway, owns a lot of Gillette stock.

King Gillette started the company in an era when men purchased straight razors for shaving. When blades dulled, they were sharpened with stroke made across a razor strop, a leather belt made for that purpose.

Razor users would cut themselves, sometimes tragically, using the razors on the market. Gillette came along and invented the safety razor, a disposable blade that fit only Gillette's razor.

If you wanted safety, you were going to use a Gillette. He captured his market for the long haul. Gillette gave the razor away free with an initial purchase of blades.

Gillette's genius was seeing that he was not in the razor business. He was in the blade business, and specifically, in the safe-shaving blade business.

Men would buy one razor and keep it for life. Gillette gave them a never ending supply of blades that men could use, toss away, and never have to sharpen.

It's fascinating that it took about fifty years for the next innovation in shaving to occur, the completely disposable plastic razor.

Once again, the key is in defining one's challenge properly, and if you are in business, defining it lucratively.

Both are eminently achievable if you ask a better question and think-through a better answer.

10

That's Impossible!

Back in the 1960s President Kennedy declared that by the end of the decade America would land a man on the moon and bring him back, safely.

This was a stunning challenge, the stuff of science fiction. At the time of this great announcement, America didn't have the technology to achieve what Kennedy had set forth.

Einstein's theories suggested when two black holes merge, the result is gravity waves are propelled through the cosmos. No one expected this far out motion to be validated or invalidated because we didn't have the instruments to detect the telltale wobbles that would be caused.

Guess, what? We do now, and recently, as you may know, scientists listened to these gravity waves that give off a distinctive sound.

The impacts of this discovery won't be known right away, but they are thought to be many and very profound.

People have made practically everything we see and use during a typical day. These items include the oaken lawyer's desk that I'm using to support my computer, the carpet beneath my feet, the house that puts a roof over my head.

This endless list of creations and inventions is boggling inasmuch as they were all conceived before they were achieved. They were thoughts before they became things.

The next time there is a power failure when you're watching a favorite program you'll be reminded of the significance of what I'm saying. We so take for granted the existence and functionality of what we are surrounded by that the miracle of these gizmos is revealed only when they dysfunction.

But they weren't here a short while ago, in geological terms. Someone had to conjure them up, to design them, to make working prototypes.

Because objects were not here, most folks couldn't imagine them appearing. They were too busy thinking about what exists to bother imagining things that do not.

Except for the few that thought, "Wouldn't it be great if we could talk across great distances, instantly?" That must have been Alexander Graham Bell's thought.

If before he set forth to invent the telephone he told people what he was working on, many would have asserted, "Why, that's impossible!"

We almost always discount the possibility of the invisible, the not yet palpable. Theory isn't something we can touch or toss back and forth like a football in the park.

It needs a manifestation before most folks will take it seriously.

For them, if you can't see it, touch it, smell it, taste it, or hear it, then it doesn't exist.

Yet, arguably, it is exactly those that are pursuing the impossible that are the ones making the world a more interesting and more useful planet for the rest.

I saw one of the world's finest actors on the London stage. It was a matinee performance and luckily I had secured a last minute ticket at the box office that placed me in about the fifth row.

At one point in the action, her character seemed to "float" across the stage. She was, in truth, walking, but the aura of defying gravity was so apparent that there seemed to be a supernatural force lifting and moving her.

Mysterious forces seem to assist performing artists, with great regularity. They have to be to produce the illusions they do, on cue.

Last weekend my family and I went to see the ballet version of Cervantes' "Don Quixote." The male lead leaped so high and so many times and with such precision as to defy the imagination.

He did the impossible, and it took everyone's breath away.

Many attend sporting events to share in the spectacular, those moments when humans seem to do what cannot be done.

When I was growing up I tried out for Little League baseball. The Dodgers selected me. The Cardinals chose my best friend, Bobby. He was a pitcher and I was a catcher.

I joked with him that the first time I faced his pitching I would hit a home run over the fence in dead center field. I was "calling my shot" as the famous Babe Ruth supposedly had done before slamming a pitch out of the park, long, long ago.

Time passed, and it didn't seem like I'd ever get my chance. Still, I kept boasting to Bobby that I would pull off this impossible feat.

He just shook his head and smirked, to signify that I was delusional.

In the middle of a game against the Cardinals, Bobby was brought in to relieve the starting pitcher. I was in the on deck circle. There were no outs recorded at that moment, so it was a certainty that we'd have our showdown, our highly anticipated gunfight at the OK Corral.

I stepped into the batter's box, stifled a broad grin, and nodded toward center field. He just shook his head as he gazed at his catcher for a sign.

Bobby threw two out of the strike zone. Then he painted the outside corner of the plate with a screwball, that trails away from the hitter and then returns to the strike zone.

I swung with all of my might, and I made contact, but because I had put so much torque into my bodily movement the ball was lost to my line of sight.

Then I looked up. It was soaring high above center field, dead center field.

It went back, back, back, and then it landed outside the fence for a home run!

Hitting a home run is an exceptional experience to begin with. All kinds of things have to happen just right to permit this to happen.

You need a pitch you can hit. Your swing has to be timed well, and you need to get the fat part of the bat on the ball.

You're trying to hit a speeding sphere with a spherical, barrel shaped object that is also moving very fast.

But this was different. I had been visualizing this perfect outcome for two years, joking about it, boasting that I would do it.

Not only that I said I'd do it my first time at bat against Bobby, and I would hit it over dead center field.

What are the odds?

If anything, Bobby had an incentive to pitch around me, to throw impossible and exotic projectiles that would deprive me of the chance to pull off the miracle.

I did the impossible, right?

To me, in my mind, it was exactly the opposite. I made that home run a certainty. I simply had to do what I said I would do, what I wanted to do, what I had imagined doing.

Pundits that are inclined to use positive thinking are fond of saying, "Anything your mind can conceive you can achieve."

Einstein is often quoted as saying "The imagination is more important than knowledge." His famous ideas about relativity came to him in a dream where he envisioned himself riding a beam of light in front of a train.

Knowledge is about what already exists. Imagination leaps far ahead of knowledge into the ineffable, the unknown and the uncharted.

It is wise to consider what Arthur C. Clarke observed about the impossible:

> *"Every revolutionary idea seems to evoke three stages of reaction. They may be summed up by the phrases: It's completely impossible, it's possible, but it's not worth doing, I said it was a good idea all along."*

Look around you. All of these creative and useful things we see and use to such great advantage were once impossible.

Let that inspire you to ignore what you see if you think it is the limit of your reach.

11

Forgiveness Dissolves Self-Contempt

I was reading about the late and distinctive actor, Sterling Hayden. Interesting fellow.

During the Second World War he served with distinction under an assumed name. From what I could surmise, he was an undercover operative in the Office of Strategic Services, the OSS.

Among other things, sailing in stealth, he smuggled weapons in an out of tight spots.

He went on to snare some major roles in movies, to write well-received novels, and to philosophize on late night TV, where he became somewhat of a fixture.

Hayden remarked that he came to deeply regret his testimony before the House Un-American Activities Committee, which was investigating Hollywood's communists.

Hayden admitted a brief membership in the communist party and then became a friendly witness, "naming names" of others that had communist affiliations.

Regarding his testimony, he would later write in his autobiography:

"I don't think you have the foggiest notion of the contempt I have had for myself since the day I did that thing."

I'm not terribly interested in the politics of that time or his specific views, but what he said about self-contempt is worth discussing because it is a form of stinking thinking worth some exploration.

Self-contempt, as Hayden was using the term, means loathing or hating one's actions. Why do we do this?

Generally, we despise ourselves when we feel our conduct belies our values.

The man whose fortunes have fallen into an abyss steals a loaf of bread to feed his children. Necessity drives him to do it.

While he sees himself as an honest bloke, and he values the commandment prohibiting theft, he can make an exception for the good of his family.

Stealing the bread might at a later date come back to him as an unfortunate deed, but it doesn't occasion self-loathing. Simply put, it isn't an act that he would not repeat if the circumstances recurred.

In Hayden's case, he may have felt his acting career was on the line, that he'd be blacklisted and never work again as an actor in Hollywood if he didn't offer testimony.

He probably came to appreciate that he wouldn't starve if he didn't act. He had options. He had lived on the seas, circumnavigating the globe several times over.

Having done courageous deeds during the war, he probably came to equate his testimony against Hollywood mates as cowardly, not befitting a real man.

But what can you do if you're Hayden? If you maintain a perfectionistic standard about what it means to be manly, if you think you always have to comport yourself heroically, you'll suffer infinite self-recriminations.

This quickly becomes counterproductive, robbing a person of the energy and focus to do good and nobler things.

How do you bridge from self-hatred to self-acceptance, from a tainted past to a clear and calm present?

First, as Dr. Albert Ellis, whom I mention elsewhere would advise, you need to change your definition of what you feel from serious shame to the lesser feeling of regret.

Instead of saying to yourself, "It's awful that I did that deed," this needs to transform into "It's regrettable I did that."

Don't get me wrong. It isn't as if you're putting a rosy gloss on your behavior. You aren't saying it is good that you turned in your friends and colleagues.

(Though an argument can be made that if you were able to "prove opposites," as Aristotle would call it, arguing that from bad came good, this might help you to alleviate your self-loathing.)

The next step is to forgive oneself. To do this you need to reduce the conflict you feel between your value system and your despised conduct.

"I'm not the only one to buckle under the pressure" might be one rationalization.

"I'm only human, and humans make mistakes," would be another mollifying thought.

I mentioned values, the preferences we maintain for conducting ourselves in the world and for choosing certain beliefs over others.

A way to avoid Hayden's predicament is to avoid self-loathing altogether, if you can. A good way to do this is to know your values and to deliberately and thoughtfully apply them to life's moments of decision.

I like the lists of values that researcher Milton Rokeach devised. Rokeach urged his students and others to rank their values from top to bottom, listing their number one, two, three most important and least important values.

By doing this values-clarification exercise, you can make decision making easier and more efficient. The process also frees you to a large extent from feeling remorse from the value conflicts that are otherwise all too easy to trip over.

Here are Rokeach's eighteen "terminal values" or desired end states, not ranked in any order of importance:

1. True Friendship
2. Mature Love
3. Self-Respect
4. Happiness
5. Inner Harmony
6. Equality
7. Freedom
8. Pleasure

9. Social Recognition
10. Wisdom
11. Salvation
12. Family Security
13. National Security
14. Sense of Accomplishment
15. World of Beauty
16. World at Peace
17. Comfortable Life
18. Exciting Life

Hayden may have felt a conflict between (3) Self-Respect and (13) National Security.

For example, soldiers may do many things in battle that are against their regular values but are justified during the exigencies of war.

Hayden could have believed that communists were a clear and present danger to the American way of life and to national security. But if he later saw this threat as a "false alarm," a form of mania or hysteria, then his self-respect value conflicted with his earlier decision and behavior.

Values tend to be somewhat enduring though they will change and sort themselves differently over time.

The single person that ranks (7) Freedom as his number one value has a dramatic change of heart after marrying and having his first child. Suddenly, (12) Family Security takes center stage where it may remain for the balance of his life as his children mature and possibly bring him grandchildren.

Value conflicts aren't all bad. When they arise, they compel us to weigh alternatives and to make thoughtful, well-considered choices.

"What really means the most to me?" we ask ourselves.

Not knowing Hayden as a person, I cannot weigh in about his religious feelings.

But some pious people might have experienced the anguish he felt over his values and behavior conflict and have responded differently.

They might have confessed what they thought was sinful behavior and have sought absolution.

They could have been told that the Almighty will judge them, and his verdict takes precedence over what mortals think.

In other words, (11) Salvation as a value could have bestowed a believer with a sense of relief and acceptance.

Self-forgiveness can enable us to let go of self-contempt and the misery it brings.

12

Beware: Visions of Slippery Slopes & Floodgates

Thanks to the miracle of TV streaming services such as Hulu and Netflix we can watch some of the most haunting and intriguing movies from yesteryear, instantly, whenever we wish.

I summoned one of these features the other night.

"The Parallax View" is a political thriller with a conspiracy theory at its heart.

A dashing reporter played by Warren Beatty is investigating a mysterious fishing death in a remote part of the Pacific Northwest.

Apparently betrayed by the local Sheriff, Beatty finds himself at the banks of a placid stream only a hundred meters from a huge dam.

The alarm sounds, warning Beatty and anyone else nearby that the floodgates are about to be opened, unleashing a huge torrent into the basin where Beatty is standing.

The floodgates do open, a deluge begins, and Beatty struggles to get traction on a slippery slope, to no avail.

He is buffeted and bruised by the rapids that seem to swallow him without a burp.

There are two metaphors in this scene that describe a nightmare scenario for anyone. "Floodgates opening" and struggling on a "Slippery slope" are vivid warnings of what can happen if we're in the wrong place at the wrong time or if we take just an initial misstep.

We can create a cascade of events and become swept up in them and not survive.

In argumentation and debate your opponent will deliberately make "floodgates" arguments to warn listeners that if we allow a trickle of your plan to be put into effect, the resulting deluge will swiftly overwhelm us.

Debaters aver to "slippery slopes" that your plan will perilously put us on. We'll lose traction, and fall into an abyss from which we won't be able to extricate ourselves.

This "In for a penny, in for a pound" thinking is frequently distorted so the persons being warned will not consent to taking the first step down a road of doom.

It's powerful rhetorical magic.

It isn't only used on us. We use it against ourselves, without conscious awareness.

Just today, in the *New York Times*, an article focused on the dietary advice that has been published over the last several decades.

Consumers have been warned against the dangers of eating butter, eggs, red meat, dairy products and other items linked to "bad cholesterol."

Millions upon millions of folks have responded to these warnings by altering their diets, radically.

Now, as this article has pointed out, much of the research that called for dramatic changes in diet has come under scrutiny.

It is currently believed that the extreme warnings weren't scientifically validated.

Articles are cropping up that say it's okay to include the "forbidden foods" in one's diet, at least in moderation.

One researcher quoted in the *Times* article said the change of focus shouldn't be seen as a green light to eat all of the double bacon cheeseburgers you want.

What he is doing is using the floodgates or slippery slope argument by implying that if people come to disbelieve what they read regarding dietary warnings, they'll lose all self-discipline and control over what they ingest.

They'll think it's open season on bingeing, that no one knows what they're talking about when it comes to healthy or unhealthy eating habits.

If it's all meaningless or ultimately contradictory research, then they'll set their own standards. And if experts permit this to happen, there's no end to the amount and kinds of foods people will eat!

People are stupid and they have no right to make free choices, without, pardon the pun, experts weighing in on what they should and should not do.

These are the silly premises that support that researcher's comment about double bacon cheeseburgers.

The problem is that we internalize what people say and imply. We come to believe the floodgates arguments.

"If I have just one filet-of-fish I'm doomed. One will lead to the next and before you know it I'll be the guy in the documentary, 'Supersize Me.' You know, the one that went on an all McDonalds diet for a month and barely survived to tell the tale!"

That belief, that an endless series of dominoes, if the first one is permitted to fall, every one thereafter will fall, is bogus, unless we believe it to be true.

And this is part of the deeper problem. The media and others teach us to think of ourselves as weak and vulnerable. Like eggshells, a mere touch and we'll fracture and fall apart.

The fact of the matter is our bodies are miraculously good at processing food, all kinds of foods.

There are people that get stranded deep inside of forests and live on nothing but tree bark until they are rescued or emerge from the thickets on their own.

No, don't go into your back yard and try this!

Of course, you won't in the same way that you'll tire of a McDonalds-only diet.

If you shut out the shouting of experts and listen to your body, you'll hear that small, sweet voice occasionally saying, "I'd like a salad for a change," or "A piece of fruit would be nice."

Consider this: It isn't the food we put into our bodies that harms us; it is the weird beliefs we foster about the foods that harm us.

I've mentioned elsewhere the power of suggestion, the fact that we are entranced and we're hypnotizing ourselves all the time.

We can hypnotize ourselves into adopting bad habits and good ones. If we convince ourselves that the foods we ingest are poisonous, we're setting ourselves up to experience indigestion and worse.

Food paranoia, I'm saying, is more of a problem than the food most of us are eating.

Fat paranoia, in the same way, is making us obsess about putting on weight.

Breaking News: Scientists are saying what we thought about BMI, the Body Mass Index, that defined over a third of the American population as obese, is now considered wrong.

What took them so long to acknowledge this obviously bogus measurement? It stated that bodybuilders, true fitness freaks, were at risk for all kinds of diseases because their combined height, weight, and gender came to a certain single number.

Everyone knows muscle weighs more than fat, except the scientists that swore by the validity of this obviously flawed statistic.

But millions of people used the BMI as a guideline and thus operated under the false belief they were obese. This judgment may have led some to eat even more, because they felt they were doomed.

Floodgates were opened, slippery slopes tripped up others, dominoes fell, and people in for pennies put on the pounds.

These things happen when we allow ourselves to believe that "one thing leads to another," and we have no control over the process.

That's stinking thinking.

When you observe your thoughts, pay special attention to this tendency to exaggerate our weaknesses. Summon the strength to dash that idea the second the thought occurs.

And for good measure, enjoy that bacon cheeseburger you've been dreaming about!

13

Devalue the Negative

Human beings are hard wired to remember the negative more than the positive.

According to at least one credible source, the adage, "Once burned, twice shy:" is a gross underestimate.

It should probably read, "Once burned, five times shy," because it takes five good happenings to offset a single misfortune.

This is odd, isn't it? As rational beings, there is no more reason to over-weigh the negative, is there?

Perhaps there is.

We have to go back to how we got here, onto this planet. The other day I read that the improbability of our being born was several trillion-to-one. We're very lucky to have arrived on this baby blue sphere, period.

How did survival happen?

A lot of our ancestors, including every one leading up to us, was a conservative, in some sense. He or she lasted long enough to sire our ancestors, and they to sire us.

In the forests, this meant they had to avoid eating those poisonous mushrooms or being gored by rampaging boars.

These dangers and others had to be pointed out to them in no uncertain terms so they could endure, procreate, and pass forward our genetic legacies.

In a word, the negatives, the "parade of horribles" as lawyers call them, all of the bad consequences that could befall a daydreamer or a thrill seeker needed to be underscored and repeated, ad nauseam.

This is why I astonish myself by automatically invoking with my children the same script my Dad used with me.

"Look both ways for traffic, then look again before crossing."

"Watch out for cars!"

"Bicycles dart out from behind that fence."

"Don't run into any joggers!"

The list is endless.

This drive for caution leads to obvious distortions. We send signals that say, "Don't take risks!"

And we imply through repeating these safety mantras that the world can be tamed, that it can be an orderly, calm, supportive place.

Sometimes this is true, until it isn't.

I just read that a school mate was mowed down by a car a block away from where I once lived. By all reports, Danny had become quite a solid citizen.

A lawyer and professor, his last post before passing was as a superior court judge.

I'm sure he was caution, incarnate. But he couldn't completely extricate himself from those omnipresent dangers that we warn our kids about.

A car struck me in a crosswalk about fifteen years ago. This morning, I noticed one of my scars.

It is on my left knee and it is the residue of a high impact that shattered a parking light on the vehicle that struck me.

To this day I cross streets with great trepidation and I try to use my sixth sense to avoid unseen dangers.

But that one bad episode that landed me in the hospital has emotionally altered thousands of subsequent street crossings for me. Psychologists would say my "illusion of safety" has been shattered.

Maybe this is a good thing, given what happened to Danny.

I have always received good-to-excellent teaching evaluations and the same can be said for feedback I've received from those that have attended my training programs at companies and speeches before associations.

What has often irked me is one person out of perhaps ten, twenty, or thirty, will bash me and bash my efforts on evaluation forms. Where the great majority praised my sense of humor, that lone misanthrope will label it, "cheesy."

Let's be rational, for a minute. We're talking about overcoming those thoughts that can be deleterious.

How much weight should I give to one person out of twenty that disliked my program? We know the adage, "You can't please all of the people all of the time," correct?

One in twenty, expressed statistically, is only 5%. If you had a business and you were able to consistently please 95% of your clients or customers you'd conclude you were fairly successful, isn't that right?

But my tendency is to dwell on that one negative evaluation, to ruminate about it.

If I were to change my approach as that one individual implied, curtailing my jokes and withdrawing the light touch, would that change actually please that person, and others like him or her?

Or was he simply looking for an excuse to criticize?

Is there some truth in Chris Jami's observation that:

"Creative people are often found either disagreeable or intimidating by mediocrities"?

In other words, I could turn myself inside out to please this grumpy soul and rob myself of the joy of delivering information in a manner most people appreciate.

And that grump would still not like me!

All of these things tell us, logically, to devalue that one unhappy camper and to focus on the huge number of the very pleased.

And I'm going to recommend this tack to you while acknowledging that it isn't so easy to do.

I believe it is our hyperactive survival mechanism that precludes us from letting go of the negatives.

That hard-wired brain of ours that remembers and emphasizes the bad senses some danger from that hostile individual, some greater risk to our well-being.

"Maybe, I'm going overboard with the humor," we could start telling ourselves.

"Perhaps I can find a way to reach this type of mal-content and disarm him, like a martial artist using ai-kido."

In a great article appearing in the *New York Times*, "Praise is Fleeting But Brickbats We Recall," (3-23-12) this topic of the persistence of negativity was explored in depth.

Let me quote from it, directly:

Roy F. Baumeister, a professor of social psychology at Florida State University, captured the idea in the title of a journal article he co-authored in 2001, "Bad Is Stronger Than Good," which appeared in The Review of General Psychology.

"Research over and over again shows this is a basic and wide-ranging principle of psychology," he said. "It's in human nature, and there are even signs of it in ani-mals," in experiments with rats.

As the article, which is a summary of much of the research on the subject, succinctly puts it: "Bad emotions, bad parents and bad feedback have more impact than good ones. Bad impressions and bad stereotypes are quicker to form and more resistant to disconfirmation than good ones."

So Professor Baumeister and his colleagues note, losing money, being abandoned by friends and receiv-ing criticism will have a greater impact than winning money, making friends or receiving praise.

In an experiment in which participants gained or lost the same amount of money, for instance, the dis-

tress participants expressed over losing the money was greater than the joy that accompanied the gain.

"Put another way, you are more upset about losing $50 than you are happy about gaining $50," the paper states.

In addition, bad events wear off more slowly than good ones.

I mentioned earlier that it takes, according to researchers, and average of five good events to offset a bad one.

One investigator said she keeps a file of positive emails that contain only praise at the ready to counteract the negative feedback she occasionally encounters.

By doing this, I say she is deliberately devaluing the negative, which is exactly what we all need to remember to do.

In this way, we, too can correct the distorting impact bad events, bad thoughts, and bad people have on us.

14

Inch-By-Inch It's A Cinch; Yard-By-Yard It's Hard!

I was working the graveyard shift at Safeway, stocking shelves.

Blasting from the loudspeakers was Beethoven's 9th symphony, the favorite of the shift supervisor. So, what was I going to say?

(Decades later, I'd come to like Beethoven's Moonlight Sonata and other pieces very much, but the 9th I can still take a pass on.)

When my shift ended, I'd run up a big hill that was the length of three city blocks. There, I'd catch a bus that took me to college. I had morning and evening classes, which made the commute and my working & sleeping cycles pretty weird.

Also, studying wasn't easy to do. I'd sandwich it into the intervals between classes. But this wasn't optimal.

I found a better way to get good grades and to learn what was being taught.

When I would sit in class I would force myself to engage in rapt attention. The walls could have fallen at my sides and I wouldn't have budged. I was locked into each syllable my teachers uttered.

And when they would mention an event, such as the war of 1812, I would hear cannons going off. I used my imagination, actively, to amplify and to make memorable what would otherwise be fairly dry facts and figures.

By taking heed of smaller and smaller units of information, and by committing them to memory at the instant I heard them, I overcame the need to do a lot of cramming for exams, which is the custom of most college students.

Instead of waiting for the 11th hour to learn what I had missed in classes, I simply didn't let anything escape my attention when I was sitting there.

Jerry Lucas, a former NBA basketball star, and Jerry Lorayne wrote a fine text called *The Memory Book*. Essentially, they endorsed what I was doing.

When you want to remember someone's name link it to some familiar or bizarre image. Let's say the last name is Linstein. That can be broken into two parts.

"Lin" looks a little like "Lion" and "Stein" looks like a beer "Stein."

So, if you put the two images together, you have a lion drinking a stein of beer. Or, you have a beer stein with a big lion for its handle.

These are practically indelible images once you conjure them. So, to remember that individual's name you just have to bring up a mental image you constructed on the spot that summons that name.

Lucas and Lorayne would go on late night TV shows and before they were introduced they would have all audience members stand-up, mention their names, and then sit down.

Later, when the authors came onto the stage they were challenged to recall each and every name, in order, which they were able to do, without forgetting any.

It seemed miraculous. Most folks fail to listen to someone's name upon being introduced. Then, they fail to associate that name with a memorable image.

So, this was the secret to my success as an undergraduate student who had to brave long working hours, an arduous commute, and scarce study time.

The thinking capability that facilitates such feats is paying attention to smaller and smaller details and then submitting them to memory.

The error in thinking that prevents us from doing this is attributable to at least a few things.

For one, nobody has shown most of us how to improve either our listening ability or how to flex our memories.

Thus, we don't think it's possible, and we simply don't try to improve in these areas.

Moreover, we're looking for big-picture shortcuts, very much like cramming for exams at the last minute. At best, the facts and figures and other data we learn in that way are committed to short-term memory, only.

If we're lucky, we'll score a passing grade on the exam, unless we are distracted by something else.

Lucas & Lorayne's method promotes longer-term memory.

To sum up the difference between the two forms of thinking it would be with this expression:

Inch by inch it's a cinch; yard by yard it's hard.

This is a crucial concept if you want to improve your thinking capacity. It goes well beyond doing memory tricks.

Many of us learn to swing for the fences in our thinking and in our subsequent behaviors. We try to hit grand-slam home runs in the bottom of the 9th inning, and trot around the bases while receiving huge applause from an adoring crowd.

Let me give you an example.

Most people want to make more money. I appreciate this and as a coach and an author I show them how. My current audio seminar, "How to Get Paid Far More Than You're Worth," taps into this theme.

How do people try to get a raise? Typically, if they're employed, they build up their courage and ask their boss for one.

This is pretty obvious, but it is an all-or-nothing "yard by yard" approach. Sometimes it works, but when it doesn't, there is no Plan "B" for most raise-seekers.

They should be reaching out to new companies and to other contacts within their current company that can grant their wishes.

By just researching and then approaching one company or person a day, by phone, by email, or by both means, a person can keep her existing job and look to hook a great big fish for her next position.

I knew a person at Time-Life who interviewed widely for other jobs while he reported to me. I didn't mind because I felt we would probably keep him and I wanted to benchmark what we were offering against the offers of other firms in the local area.

He received a ton of job offers!

Partly, this was the result of having a devil-may-care attitude about what he was doing. He was simply experimenting, and letting his curiosity lead him to positions that he wasn't remotely qualified for.

His take it or leave it attitude made him an even more desirable catch.

Inch by inch he got multiple offers, including some that frankly exceeded ours at Time-Life.

If he had focused on asking me, his boss, I would have simply said, "Barry, if you want more pay, then sell more books!"

Whatever your objective is, break it down into smaller and smaller units that you can manage with very little effort.

Don't fall into the trap of thinking that every initiative requires huge, super-human effort to achieve.

Concern yourself with the inches and you'll see the yards will take care of themselves!

15

Stop Second-Guessing Yourself

At 19, after doing a lot of menial jobs at restaurants and other companies, I rose in the ranks to become the best salesperson Time-Life had.

So it didn't come as a surprise to me when the sales manager left to open the Chicago office that I would get the nod to replace him.

I liked everything about the position. The pay was good. The hours were long, but somehow I was able to sandwich in my college classes, which were located just a few miles away.

And I liked the responsibility of recruiting, interviewing, hiring, supervising and compensating not only salespeople but also the customer service and collections team.

But the transition into management wasn't without a snag or two.

One stickler was Bud.

Bud was the second-best seller on the staff, after me. We were always competing for bonuses and recognition.

I usually earned more distinctions, which progressively unnerved him.

And then my big promotion came. I was no longer expected to sell. I needed to get others to sell well, and of course, because I was promoted, I had to replace my sales production.

Bud could do better than he was doing. And since I took over, he pouted and under-performed. I believe he wanted to make me look bad and out of my depth as a leader.

If he could destabilize my new regime, he could take over after toppling me.

I called him into my office and laid it on the line.

"Bud I need more production from you. You also need to be a good role model, and stop goofing-off."

He just sat there, smirking. It was clear this was one fellow that wasn't on my team. He was out for himself.

"Bud, shape-up, or we're going to have a different conversation."

He didn't.

I called him in again and I fired him.

Naturally, our sales tanked on the day I let him go. My boss phoned in for the numbers as was his custom.

"What happened?" he asked breathlessly.

"Bud is no longer with us."

"He quit?"

"No, I had to fire him."

Nervously, I explained that he was depressing sales. I would bring in new hires, train them well, and he would shoot them down by lording it over them.

"Sales will perk up," I promised.

Not totally convinced, Larry, my boss said, gravely, "Well, I just hope you're right!"

To my credit, I worked like a dog to make things right. I put extra effort into training and coaching my newer people. I did demonstrations. I nearly walked on my hands to get them to outperform expectations.

And they responded. Within a month, our sales had climbed to the pre-firing of Bud point.

After that, they kept getting better and better. We doubled the staff and set records for sales achievement.

This is actually a good story with a happy ending. What's critical here is Larry may have second-guessed the personnel decision that I made.

But I didn't second-guess myself.

Second-guessing yourself is a very bad habit. "If I had only done X instead of Y," you tell yourself, "Everything would have turned out better."

What we experience when we second-guess is something psychologists term, *post-decisional dissonance.*

Imagine a set of scales. Your decision may have gone either way. In this case, the scales would have been even. Or possibly there was more evidence to support the decision you made.

When you second-guess, you put more support on the side of the un-chosen alternative. This causes psychological pain and discomfort.

How can you avoid second-guessing? There are several ways.

First of all, you can learn to trust yourself more often. At 19, I trusted my instincts. I "read" Bud as a dud, someone that would never be a team player, at least on my squad.

I had captained so many sports teams before Bud came along that I trusted my instincts. If I had to pick a team from scratch, I'd simply never choose him.

Another thing you can do is to get comfortable with making mistakes. "What's the worst thing that could happen?" is a great question to ask yourself.

In the Bud case, the worst is that I'd be de-selected from management and put back in the sales bullpen. No worries there, I ruled it before and I'd be on top, again.

Also, ask yourself if your decision matches your fundamental values. Mine did. I valued achievement and I asked Bud for his, which he refused to deliver. I put him on notice and he persisted in his under-performance.

I wasn't asking him to do anything I wouldn't do. Indeed, I had put out 100% as a sales rep and I was doing the same as a manager. So, I wasn't being hypocritical.

I knew Bud was a capable seller who would quickly be grabbed by another company. But he had reached the end of the line with ours, and he was probably waiting for an excuse to depart.

Peter F. Drucker has said many times in my presence, "No one is really good at hiring people." I infer he would have said the same about measuring their performance and terminating them, as well.

You've probably heard the adage that the only people that don't make mistakes are the people that don't contribute anything at all.

But inactivity is an even bigger mistake than making mistakes!

We need to take a "Win some, lose some" attitude toward most things.

As one person said, "Make a decision and then make that decision right!"

If it doesn't turn out to be 100% great, live with it if it cannot be undone.

Comfort yourself in belief that everything that doesn't work out can serve as a lesson. But don't spend too much time looking for lessons before jumping back into the arena.

In my book, *Dr. Gary S. Goodman's 77 Best Practices In Negotiation* I share some of my deals-gone-bad, in the final chapter. If there is a unifying theme, something that I have learned from these mistakes it is this:

Better to have done an imperfect deal than to have waited to do more perfect ones.

I have left a small fortune on the table from agreements that I walked away from because I second-guessed their quality and desirability.

Boxer Jake LaMotta who was coached by his brother didn't want to accept a bout against a higher-ranked fighter. His brother, who realized what was really at stake at that point in the pugilist's career said:

"Take the fight because if you win you win and if you lose you win."

In other words, do it and don't look back or second-guess yourself. That's sage advice!

16

"You'll Never Learn English!"

Stinking thinking isn't limited to the thoughts we originate in our own minds.

All too frequently, these debilitating notions come from other people. Bombarded by their dismal and dour notions, we take them on as our own.

Repeating them to us, and then repeating them to ourselves, we adopt these ideas but seldom consciously appreciate that they're aliens.

They don't belong to us, unless we become aware of their provenance and we deliberately cast them aside.

I was speaking to an immigrant the other day. Her English isn't perfect, but it is still passable, and occasionally very good.

She is still expanding her vocabulary, and she enjoys becoming more competent in this, her second language.

But when she was in school back in her homeland, she started her English language education. She had the misfortune to study with a poisonous teacher.

The teacher told her student straight-out: "You'll never learn English!"

This was such a stark and negative conclusion that the young woman couldn't blot it out.

But of course it had a pernicious effect. Every time the young lady would try to master an aspect of English that nasty voice echoed in her mind.

"I'll never learn English!"

And worse, this self-statement was accompanied by, "So, why bother trying?"

As life would have it, the woman immigrated to the United States, where of course the official language is English. Now, she had no choice but to master the language.

Her employment depended on it. Her friendships depended on it. Her self-esteem, to a large extent, depended on it.

Unfortunately, it hasn't been easy.

She takes no little glee in the fact that she has been proving that caustic teacher wrong. Sometimes, she'll even bellow, "Here I am; a person that will NEVER learn English!"

But the pain remains, beneath the joke.

The fact is that stinking thinking is often imposed on us.

I remember sitting in the back seat of the family car as my mother went on errands with her girlfriend at the time, another mom.

That person would occasionally say about me, "He's so quiet back there!" as if my silence was symptomatic of something beyond politeness or shyness.

Later I learned this woman was something of a speech therapist. She was constantly on the hunt for people that suffered from defective diction.

In a word, she was always trawling for business, so it paid her to uncover and to exploit symptoms of poorly formed words.

Of course, all of this backstage manipulation was well beyond the powers of a kid no older than five to appreciate or to protect himself from.

Once, with a great sense of alarm she turned around and asked my mother in a challenging tone, "Is he breathing through his MOUTH?"

This completely flummoxed me. I hadn't paid much attention to the orifices I used for this essential activity. But this person was bent on making me conscious of it, or to be more precise, she made me instantly self-conscious about breathing.

Now, I know she made many errors, one of which was discussing her observations in my presence.

Gratefully, my mother didn't take the bait. I wasn't admonished to change my respiration habits, and as I matured in due course I suppose I became less of a mouth-breather.

I even went on to teach speech communication at the university level for five years and to become a well-paid professional public speaker. I suppose all traces of my purported "malady" were completely gone by that point.

When others make you self-conscious, become instantly aware of it. They are probably implanting a negative thought in your mind that has no rightful place echoing inside of it.

Sometimes these negatives can be disguised as compliments, but they have the same sort of deleterious effects.

I was 12 and in my final year of Little League baseball, which I loved. I was having a pretty good year and I was the captain of my team.

One day, about two thirds of the way through the season, a very excited president of the league dashed up to me and said hello. I knew his son, and they were neighbors.

He said, "Do you know how well you're doing?"

I had no idea what he was talking about.

"Do you know what you're HITTING?" he clarified.

"No, I don't," I replied in truth.

I suppose that was a little unusual for a kid. I knew the batting averages of my favorite major leaguers, and I had a sense of my batting averages during Little League years past.

But I guess I was so absorbed in life as we know it and in the season that I was participating in at the moment to be oblivious about my exact level of statistical contribution.

"You're hitting .638, and I already checked with Williamsport about what you did the other day. It's a record. You pitched the game, hit three home runs in it, and during your prior at bat in the last game you also hit a homer!"

"Oh," I think I said, not knowing what to make of this flurry of facts and their implications.

I'm not going to tell you that my batting average tanked after that chat. I finished the year hitting .582, which is still extremely rare and impressive.

That earned me a gold medal as the best hitter in the league.

I came in second in total home runs and I was made captain of the all-star team.

But I do recall something changed inside of me. I liked the praise and the recognition, but I also felt stressed by the notoriety and the buzz.

People in the stands, including my Dad, felt they weren't just watching another 12 year old and neighbor but someone that was destined to break records in baseball for the rest of his life.

There was even talk about how a scout from the New York Mets looked me over at one of my games.

Hitting adolescence, I just wanted to be left alone, and while I liked baseball I never played it with the same enthusiasm as I had before, when it was just what I did without self-consciousness.

In fact, the moment I stopped doing it for me and started feeling I had a duty to do it for other people, it became a source of discomfort instead of personal satisfaction.

Looking back at the three examples I just discussed, which I'll refer to as: "You'll never learn English," "There's something amiss about your breathing," and "You're a superstar ballplayer," there is a common thread.

In each, we have a person observing us from their narrow perspective. They're promoting a definition of us that is satisfactory to them, but which makes us self-conscious. And this self-consciousness robs us of the ability to own each moment of our lives, ourselves.

If you are a parent and people in authority offer an opinion of your child that is distorted or self-serving, call them on it.

If you are an adult and the same thing happens to you, call them on it.

Don't let these intrusive notions take root. See them for what they are, and deliberately toss them aside.

17

Every Day In Every Way You're Getting Better & Better!

In other sections, I mentioned Dr. Philip Zimbardo, whom I hold in high regard as a psychologist, researcher, and author.

At age 76, he said he never felt happier in his life. And I believe him!

He attributes his good cheer to balancing his thoughts in time. He has his mind planted properly in three time zones: the past, present and future. He remembers the best from his past, is busy with research and writing today, and he holds out hope for the future.

His description of happiness is quite at odds with most other people of his vintage. Many of them complain constantly and believe strongly that today is inferior to yesterday, and tomorrow will be worse.

Even more significantly, they tell themselves and others their powers are in steep decline and they aren't nearly as effective or desirable as they were in days gone by.

I believe they are making whatever objective situation they are in far worse than it needs to be. And they are probably talking themselves into an early grave.

It is a psychological fact that we are being hypnotized constantly. We are also hypnotizing ourselves.

In American society pharmaceutical products dominate television and many other forms of advertising. The constant drumbeat is that something is wrong with us. We must find out what it is and we desperately need the medications being offered to alleviate its symptoms.

If it weren't so tragic, you could make a laugh-out-loud comedy out of simply reading the side effects that fast-talkers race through at the end of ads. In most cases, the treatments sound far worse in their effects than the maladies they are aimed at relieving.

Contrast the way pharmaceuticals are sold today with how French pharmacist Emile Coue packaged them in the 1920s, in France.

Coue wrote small notes to patients that talked-up the benefits of the treatments and prognosticated that the users would return to full health in record time.

What is astounding is the fact that many did just that. They regained functionality so fast that word of his miracle cures spread.

Coue had discovered the placebo effect, the power of suggestion. He encouraged the use of autosuggestion by his patients. A famous line of his, which later was brought to the United States by authors such a Norman Vincent Peale and Robert Schuller is:

Every day in every way I'm getting better and better!

The concept is to repeat this phrase multiple times during the morning, afternoon and evening. You'll hypnotize yourself into believing this to be true, and it will become true for you.

If you are ill, your symptoms may subside. If you are feeling blue, your spirits will become upbeat again.

Certainly this won't work for certain people and some maladies are too dire to respond to autosuggestion. But Coue's results were nothing less than astonishing.

Let's get back to people's beliefs about aging. If you keep telling yourself, every day in every way I get worse and worse, are you likely to get better and better?

Of course, not! You'll reap what you sow.

There is a popular expression today about the power of intention. It simply says, "You get what you think about."

If you think about winning, you'll win; and if you think about losing, you'll lose, all other things being equal.

We move in the direction of our predominant thoughts.

As I've said many times during our time together you should examine your thoughts. What are you telling yourself, especially about your health and fitness?

Are you over the bend and beyond repair? If you keep repeating this idea, you'll feel that way.

But let's say you're 80 years old, 85, or even 95. You do realize that there are hundreds of millions of people in China that are fit and supple at those ages. They do Tai Chi, the gentle martial art.

They can be seen in parks across the land. Deliberately, they are building up their "chi" or life force.

Everyday in every way they're getting stronger and stronger.

Every day in every way they're getting more and more flexible, and less and less brittle.

What about you?

Are your thoughts predicting gloom and doom or sunshine and success?

It's your choice. Coue's method points to the fact that we are either programming ourselves to live a healthy life or we are programming ourselves to be incapacitated by diseases, real and imagined.

What is your choice?

Every day in every way I'm getting sicker and sicker or every day in every ways I'm getting healthier and healthier.

Select an affirmation and repeat it to yourself.

I'll tell you one that has worked miracles for me:

Every day in every way I'm richer and richer!

I remember excitedly telling a family member, "We're rich!"

She said, "We are?"

And I went on to explain I had this feeling everything would work out well in my business. I was implementing a promising plan and beginning to execute it. And while the results weren't in yet, I was predicting, just like they declare a winner on election night with only one percent of the vote tallied, based on the early returns, we're rich!

That fact wouldn't become manifested until a few more years had transpired, but that didn't stop me from repeating every day these two words:

We're rich!

Not only did my thoughts and my lips say it. My mind believed it.

Then it was simply a matter of manifesting that feeling into full blossom so the objective world mirrored my rosy thoughts.

I challenge you!

Write down five areas that you believe are in decline for you. These could relate to health, wealth, relationships, learning, or to any other area.

You are telling yourself that these areas are getting worse and worse.

Now, write down their opposites.

Every day in every way such-and-such is getting better and better.

Suspend your disbelief that this won't work. Tell yourself it will work.

Repeat these affirmations several times during the course of each day for thirty days.

Check your results. What improvements do you see?

I think you'll be impressed.

18

I'm Too Young, I'm Too Old,
& I'm Too Fill-In-The-Blank

I took a feature writing class in my first year of college. As part of the course we learned a little about placing our articles in various publications.

The assigned book for this purpose was issued each year, *Writer's Digest.*

It listed thousands of publishers of not only feature articles but also books and poetry.

That last category caught my attention. I liked poetry but never wrote any, certainly not for publication.

Instead of calculating the odds of getting anything published, I plunged in.

In an hour or two I crafted two poems. On top of that I invested maybe another half hour in polishing them.

Wow, that was quick, I remember telling myself. Then the naysayer in me started to chip away at my achievement.

I thought, "That was too easy," and "Real poets struggle long and hard before they get anything into print."

And I added for good measure, "Who am I to think anyone will take me seriously? Heck, I'm only 18!"

I went back to *Writer's Digest*. I saw two publications that caught my eye and looked like they would be great outlets for my new works: *Bachaet* and *Poetry Parade*.

"Nothing attempted, nothing gained!" I encouraged myself. I invested in two pre-stamped envelopes and sent the poems off for consideration.

Shortly after that, I went on to other classes and other interests, forgetting about my submissions.

But then, one by one, I was notified that my poems were accepted for publication.

"I don't believe it!" I told myself. "This is too good to be true; what's the catch?"

One publication offered no money, only a free copy or two of the published poem.

The other paid nothing, as well, but if your poem appeared you were entered into a contest that if you won you would then be paid a nice reward.

Here I was, instead of being thrilled about getting my name and words into print, I was actively trying to snatch defeat from the jaws of victory. I just had to find the bad part of a good situation.

Of course, at the basis of my discomfort with such instant success was the corrosive thought I kept repeating to myself, if only tacitly and unconsciously: "But I'm too young!"

I don't think it really dawned on me until later that these publications had no idea whatsoever as to my age or the ages of other poets. This was actually a good thing!

Still in high school, comedian and filmmaker, Woody Allen, started his writing career by submitting his short jokes and one-liners to a New York columnist.

Before he knew it, he became highly sought-after, and he made a remarkably good income for a pipsqueak. After writing for a lot of other people his agent urged him to do some stand-up comedy in nightclubs.

He was noticeably uncomfortable, but after a while he developed confidence and a unique style that audiences liked.

Interviewed for a documentary about his life and career, he pointed out that he has been working continuously at his craft since high school.

I didn't know this about him when I sent off my poems. I should have known better than to second-guess the acceptance I was achieving.

Famously, Woody Allen quipped, "I wouldn't want to join a club that would have me as a member!"

Oddly, I felt exactly the same about gaining admission to those poetry publications.

And truth be told, I have published more than 15 books and thousands of articles in my life, but I never submitted or published a poem after that early success I reached and then spurned.

We might rightly be upset by the ageism that is in the world. People don't get proper consideration for jobs and other opportunities because of stereotypes associated with age.

But the worst ageism, I would suggest, is between our ears!

We prevent us from doing things more than outside forces do.

What are you telling yourself right now about your age? More to the point, what are you preventing yourself from doing because you are using your age as an excuse?

If you were ten or twenty years younger or older what would you consider as a proper activity that you are discounting or avoiding altogether, now?

I wrote a book and recorded an audio program titled, *The 40+ Entrepreneur.*

It shows people who are in that age bracket how to successfully start a business of their own.

I begin the program by dashing certain age myths, especially the one that says I'm too old to do this or that.

Colonel Sanders, the founder of Kentucky Fried Kitchen, KFC, was a retiree scraping by on a paltry social security check before he offered his tasty poultry recipe to the public.

Of course, his recipe caught on and he became a multi-millionaire and a great role model in the process. Who says one cannot start a huge enterprise at an advanced age?

The media are fond of publicizing the exploits of 20-something entrepreneurs that come up with the latest technology or application. But the fact of the matter is people over 35 start most new businesses, according to the *Business Insider.*

They are also well prepared to succeed by dint of their life and business experiences. Plus they often have contacts that can help them to find investment capital and management know-how.

So the fact is that it is probably incorrect for practically anyone to say he is over the hill and it is too late to start a business.

In many occupations you get far better and more effective as you age. Many of my best professors were in their 80's when I took courses with them. And under their guidance I did some of my finest work.

These luminaries include management sage, Peter F. Drucker, with whom I did my MBA.

I also studied with Dr. Albert Ellis, whom I have mentioned elsewhere in this program. He was voted by the American Psychological Association as one of the three most influential psychologists of the 20th century, and of course his influence carries on well into the 21st.

Donald C. Bryant, the Professor Emeritus from the University of Iowa and Distinguished Visiting Professor, was a key influence and mentor in the Ph.D. program I completed at the University of Southern California.

All were in their 80's, and they imparted much, because they had much to impart, and I am a lucky beneficiary of their wisdom.

It is common and all too easy to tell ourselves we're too young or too old for something. But it also becomes, from an objective standpoint, less correct as time passes.

We live in a time when people mature faster. The onset of adolescence comes sooner and sooner across cultures. Biologically at least, this makes us more competent in certain ways.

And we know life expectancy is increasing dramatically, as well. In developed countries, people are typically living into their 70s, 80s, and beyond.

I've heard of folks that are 100 that still play tennis three times per week.

Try telling them they are "too old!"

When you catch yourself succumbing to the thought that you are tool young or too old, especially if it is preventing you from being fully engaged, stimulated, or happy, question its truth.

Probably there are many folks at your exact age and beyond that are doing what you believe, falsely, it is too early or late to do.

My sister once said to me, "Gary in life people will tell you you're either too young or you're too old. This means there's never a right time to do anything! Don't believe them."

Sage advice, this is, and I offer it to you. Do every age defying thing you can imagine doing, while using your age as an opportunity and not as an obstacle.

19

"Money Is The Root Of All Evil"

Money is pervasive in all modern societies.

You can't drive down the street in many places without seeing prices for various goods and services being advertised.

I know to the penny what certain gas stations were charging for fuel, yesterday. I pay attention not only because the prices are posted, but the cost of gas is constantly referred to in the media.

Our opinion regarding the cost of fuel is much more important than its price.

If we look at the total cost of driving, what we pay for gas is fairly minor. Indulge me for a minute, and I'll explain.

Let's say you buy a car for $25,000. Your monthly payment on a four-year loan will probably be around $600 a month. You'll pay about $150 a month in insurance.

Oil changes and tires and maintenance will also average about $100 a month if nothing major breaks.

And then we have depreciation. This is what your car loses in value as you use it, putting on miles, and simply as it ages. After four years you'll be lucky if your car sells for half of what you paid: $12,500.

So, what you'll be out of pocket in depreciation will be $12,500 divided over 48 months, that's another $260.42 per month.

Adding your monthly payments, insurance, maintenance, and depreciation the figure totals $1,110.42.

Let's compare this figure with what you're paying for gas. We know gas fluctuates so I am going to factor in the highest I've seen it over the last decade. That's $5 per gallon.

If you drive an average of 12,000 miles per year and your car gets 20 miles per gallon, you need to buy 600 gallons of gas. That will cost you $3,000 per year.

Divided by 12, that's $250 per month that you'll be out of pocket. Add $250 to the former total for the other items and your monthly driving expense comes to a grand total of $1,360.42.

The gasoline portion of that figure is $250 divided into $1,360.42, or 18.38%.

What we see here is the fact that gasoline is a minor portion of the overall cost of driving. It could shoot up to $6 per gallon or drop to $1 per gallon, and while that might cost or save us some money, the other costs of driving are still the lion's share.

You might be scratching your head, thinking something is wrong with my figures. Straight out of college I worked in the car leasing business. Believe me when I say these numbers are fairly close to the mark.

What we pay for gas is a very minor portion of what we pay, overall, to operate a car.

Our belief about gas, however, paints an entirely different picture.

The picture in our head distorts the reality we experience in reality. When we see gasoline spiking, as it did recently in California because of some explosions in refining plans that took them offline, we howl.

Why aren't we complaining about depreciation? At $260.42, that's costing us more than gas in our hypothetical example. For that, we're only out of pocket $250 a month if we put an average amount of miles on our cars and we're paying $5 per gallon.

I alluded earlier to one of the main reasons we are price sensitive about gas and not about depreciation. The cost of fuel is posted practically everywhere so it is conspicuous to us when it goes up or down, which is almost incessantly.

The value of our car is also fluctuating practically every day based on local, regional, and national trends. Unless we're in the auto business, buying, selling, and appraising cars every day, we're completely unaware of these changes.

Only when we trade in that car or truck or try to sell it ourselves are we confronted with the reality of its value at that moment.

I saw a comedy in which a neighbor boasted about the great gas mileage he was getting from his super-efficient new car. As a prank a guy living next to him who was tired of this boasting secretly added gas to the neighbor's tank, every night.

This made the neighbor think be was beating world records for mileage. He was euphoric. The prankster suddenly changed course. He stared siphoning gas out of the car every night.

The owner went from elation to depression within 24 hours.

Not a nice thing to do with your neighbor's head, but it stands for the notion that our belief about something's value and its actual performance can be distorted.

Sidney Lecker, MD, wrote a very interesting book that I believe is out of print. If you can track down a copy, it will shed light on what I'm saying.

The book is titled, *The Money Personality*. What I got out of it is the very important point that we carry around false beliefs about money. Many of these were handed down to us in our families. Others we have soaked in from the culture to which we belong.

Lecker points to probably the granddaddy of all false money beliefs, "Money is the root of all evil."

People say this is a direct quote from the Bible. But a closer examination reveals, as the minister Catherine Ponder says in her book, *The Dynamic Laws of Prosperity*, the passage says something else.

It actually says, the WORSHIP of money is the root of all evil. If money is your idol, and you are beholden to it, Ponder says you may very well encounter some problems in your life, not unlike King Midas.

The belief that money is evil will keep you from amassing it. Lecker and Ponder say it is very unlikely you'll grow rich if you are hostile toward this substance.

This passage, and others like it, limit aspirations and productivity.

Examine your predominant thoughts about money. Challenge the ones that may be keeping you from prospering.

I think you'll find some that are holding you back!

20

What Time Zone
Are You Thinking In?

Over the last year I've been tracking my high school classmates at a web site dedicated to our graduation class.

Occasionally, the comments have been very insightful dealing with geopolitical issues. But for the most part, the notes have been trivial and even ridiculous.

I've eliminated some of my former comments, which gratefully can be accomplished at any time with the delete button. And I've decided to be more sparing in the moments I devote to the blog.

As you might expect from grown-up classmates, some of their attention is placed firmly in the past. We share the perception that our town, while sophisticated for its time, was also very much like a village when we grew up there.

Comments also are directed to the present. People banter about what's going on in the world and mention what their kids are doing.

What is missing, however, is any talk about my classmates' personal futures. What are their aims and goals?

How are they going to set the world on fire?

These were concerns at 17 and 18, when we passed around our high school yearbooks, wishing each other well, commenting on their burning desires at the time.

Certainly, some of us have realized those early ambitions. We are what we are, lawyers, doctors, professors, artists and miscellaneous other things. Hopes and dreams change, informed by how the world adjusts to us and we to the world.

All of this is a given.

But what is next for these people?

The answer is there is no next for too many of them. At least they've not revealed a future goal, a beacon that is drawing them to a particular place.

This is very sad. To be fully adjusted and fully functioning people, we need to occupy three time zones, correctly, according to Stanford's Philip Zimbardo.

Some of our thoughts should pertain to the past, and he says, specifically we need to be "past positive." Rediscover the good things that happened, your accomplishments.

There are trophies you won that have gathered dust. Take a cloth to them. Shine them up.

Relish the good that you've contributed and the good you have received, in turn.

But enough is enough. Don' allow more than a minor part of your consciousness be informed by what you can see in the rearview mirror. Appreciate that whatever you look for in the past, you'll probably find.

If you believe you had a miserable youth, there's probably evidence to support that idea. On the other hand, if you believe those days were filled with glory, you'll access a highlight reel of tape busting finishes at track meets and grand slam home runs that you stroked.

A lot of writing is about the present, especially by fans of Zen and Eastern philosophies. The idea is that "All we have is the now," so it's foolish to not be fully present for the present, so to speak.

Baba Ram Das, the former Richard Alport, wrote a classic book that sums up this notion and also provides a marching order. Its title is: *Be Here Now.*

He and others refer to the "pleasantness of presentness," the good that comes from focusing oneself in the here and now.

Want to be happy? It is not likely to happen at some distant point when you have accomplished all of your goals, according to the present-oriented gurus. You'll be likely to arrive at the destination you have charted and the waters will be shallower or choppier or simply less blue and sparkling than you had imagined.

And guess, what? At that point you'll also be experiencing a present moment, but your beingness won't be there with you. You'll be in clover, but as Dostoyevsky said, the clover won't be good enough.

Happiness is a "right now" phenomenon. Ram Dass might have said, be happy now.

A certain amount of our awareness needs to be dedicated to the present moment.

And to the extent that we can immerse ourselves in it, we can have peak experiences leaving us feeling refreshed.

Csikzentmihalyi wrote a book about people that have blissful experiences. They get into a mental state that he calls *Flow*, which is also the title of one of his books on the subject.

There is no separation between who they are and what they're doing. Sometimes, when I write or lecture I find myself in this state. Words effortlessly come to be and thoughts take on lives of their own.

Like a river, they cascade, they flow easily and inexorably toward a destination.

Ballplayers talk about being in the zone and locked-in when they give their best performances. Every move feels completely natural, and the results and victories seem to take care of themselves.

There's no performance anxiety. Concerns about "This pitch won't work" or "We can't win this game" never enter their consciousness. They would cause friction , and friction impedes flow.

You cannot be stuck in the past or shifted completely into the future and experience flow. You need to be where you are, now.

But we cannot have peak experiences 24/7. There is no such thing as eternal and ever-present bliss on the human plane.

Being able to devote one's consciousness at least temporarily to the present is needed to accomplish a lot of tasks and to enjoy their accomplishment.

But we cannot get stuck in the present.

We need to have some consciousness dedicated to the future, according to Zimbardo.

Those that accomplish the most in life are able to delay gratification and to sacrifice current pleasures for future goals. And the world-beaters, the competitors in almost every human arena are those that are predominantly future oriented.

But are they happy?

Doris Drucker, a scientist and the spouse of Peter F. Drucker, said no. Having studied the success of corporate chief executive officers, she said these folks typically had unhappy family lives and higher divorce rates than those that could "leave the office at the office" at the end of day.

But some focus on the future, perhaps fostering a little hope about what you, your family, or humanity might accomplish in the years and decades to come is needed to be completely fulfilled.

Get these thinking time zones right, balance them properly, and you might find as Zimbardo did, at age 76, that he was "happier than ever."

21

Stop Victimizing Yourself
By "Awfulizing"

For the last three seasons the Los Angeles Dodgers have won the Western Division of the National League in Major League Baseball.

This put them into the postseason. They were matched-up with other division winners and wild card teams.

The euphoria was temporary. They lost.

The Dodgers haven't won a World Series since 1988. You might say some fans are restless.

Older supporters wonder if they're going to see another Dodger World Series in their lifetimes. Many younger fans have never seen one.

There are hardcore fans that write about their feelings in the Comments section of the *Los Angeles Times* sports pages. Some are zealots.

One fellow, whose handle is Laker Fan, only publishes positive remarks. Some suspect he is a management shill, on the Dodgers' payroll because his remarks are almost always saccharine sweet and upbeat.

Others are dour and dreary, dreading the season to come. They are especially ticked off because management allowed a Western Division rival, the Arizona Diamondbacks, to snare one of the very best Dodger pitchers of the past few years, Zack Greinke.

Greinke was on the short list to receive the league's Cy Young award, the most honorific achievement for a pitcher in baseball.

How and why the Dodgers forwent re-signing Zack is not totally mysterious. Arizona paid him more money and offered a longer contract than the Dodger management said they were willing to offer.

A billionaire ownership group controls the Dodgers. They are sitting on a TV contract worth a reported $8 billion dollars. They have raised ballpark prices, and the team is profitable.

They could have paid Greinke's price, and without him they are unlikely to win the Division and even less likely to advance in the postseason if they do.

Many fans are outraged. They simply won't let go of the fact that Greinke will be pitching for a rival. For these supporters, management's actions are the sports equivalent of treason.

You can tell from their comments that these Dodger "faithful" as they call themselves are really in pain. They can't stand the idea that management, which has only been intact for a few years, is disabling the team by trading and allowing key players to depart.

I agree with them that the management staff is filled with people that seem to consistently make boneheaded decisions. I also predict the Dodgers will come in second or third place in the division.

But my approach is to monitor my thinking about all of this. Following this team for me is just a hobby. It isn't an obsession.

When I feel I am crossing a line from disappointment in their results to something Dr. Albert Ellis called, "awfulizing," then I'm using stinking thinking. Awfulizing is a sign that I am overly identified with their performance, feeling good when they win, and bad when they don't.

I consciously decide to distance myself from the team and its antics.

This means I stop reading the *Los Angeles Times* sports pages, for one thing. I go cold turkey on commenting.

Awfulizing, I tell myself, really does nothing to change the behavior of the Dodgers front office. Their President of Baseball Operations and General Manager don't reform their behavior when I print disparaging comments, however valid they may be.

I remind myself when my thinking becomes too incensed that I'm not being paid for my opinion. This is a particularly important thought because as a professional consultant I am paid for my ideas, judgment, and even predictions.

When you start to awfulize about anything, such as the too loud voice of a fellow employee in the next cubicle, calm yourself down. Appreciate you are in control of your emotions.

Here is the type of three-part logic we use when we awfulize. We tell ourselves:

I feel awful whenever the Dodgers trade or lose a great player.

The Dodgers just lost Zack Greinke to the Arizona Diamondbacks.

Therefore, I feel awful.

Dr. Ellis suggests changing the "awful" word to "mildly disappointed." So, here is the emotional logic, transformed:

I feel mildly disappointed whenever the Dodgers trade or lose a great player.

The Dodgers just lost Zack Greinke to the Arizona Diamondbacks.

Therefore, I feel mildly disappointed.

Disappointment is typically temporary and superficial. You're mildly disappointed when you don't find a parking space the first time you circle the block.

Another spot will open up or you'll settle for grabbing a space a little farther away.

If you're always running late and today you absolutely have to be on time, say to catch a plane, then it is tempting to awfulize about not seeing a parking spot right away.

Yet if you keep telling yourself it's awful, you'll elevate your blood pressure and send alarm signals to other parts of your body and to your brain.

You'll release fight-or-flight hormones. They are supposed to be deployed only in true emergencies.

Your driving will become erratic and you'll cut in front of other cars.

Instead of coping well with your circumstances you'll be telling yourself they are intolerable.

You'll be in the thick of things but be trying to escape them.

At that moment of distress you actually need to slow down, and this applies to the rate of your thinking.

You need to change that belief that "It's awful to be late" or "It's awful to miss a plane," to "Lateness happens," and "If I have to, I'll catch then next flight out."

The worst teams in baseball win about one in every three games. The very best teams win six games out of every ten, just short of two of every three games.

All other teams fall somewhere in the middle. Many win half of their games. Occasionally, one of these teams will make it to the postseason because it becomes the champion of a very weakly performing division.

And if it is lucky enough and everything falls into place, improbable as it may be, a mediocre team could advance this way to the World Series and even win it.

Motivational speaker Les Brown gives a talk that he has delivered on public television. The theme of the talk is "It's Possible."

It's possible the Dodgers will rise above the ineptitude of their current management and ownership. It's possible you'll find that parking space on the next pass.

It's possible the plane you are taking will be delayed and you'll arrive at the airport in plenty of time.

Instead of dreading that court appearance you have to defend your speeding citation, remind yourself it's possible that police officer will be sick or detained on that day, so your speeding ticket will be cancelled.

The odds of that happening where I live are one-in-three; not bad at all.

By the way, you do know where the term sports "fan" came from? Not from ceiling fans, I assure you.

It came from the word, fanatic, which is "a person marked or motivated by an extreme, unreasoning enthusiasm," according to the dictionary.

When you find yourself having extreme and unreasonable thoughts about practically anything, you're in stinking thinking territory.

Get some perspective by changing your thoughts from "awful" to "mildly disappointing."

Over the long haul, you'll probably have more fun following your sports teams, even if you aren't a die-hard "fan."

22

Monitor Your Short Term & Long Term Thinking

Psychologist Philip Zimbardo of Stanford has done extensive research on people that succeed and those that fail.

One of his findings is that those that succeed are at least slightly more future time oriented than present time oriented.

For example, he studied children that were offered a choice between taking one marshmallow right away, or if they would wait a few minutes, they would receive two.

Two-thirds of these kids grabbed that first marshmallow, foregoing the pleasure of getting two.

When the one and two marshmallow receiving kids were later studied as adults, it was determined that those that waited to get two treats, the one-third of participants, were far more successful in life than the two-thirds that couldn't resist temptation.

It has been well established that postponement of gratification is an essential ingredient in achieving worldly success. One needs to be able to forego short-term pleasures to gain disproportionate satisfactions later on.

The expression, "No pain, no gain" nicely sums up this proposition. As some pundits joke, "Success only comes before work in the dictionary."

There is something happening in the minds of those that are able to wait for their goodies. They are able to imagine or at least to infer a desired future state, in other words, a larger goal than what the present is providing. That goal must seem attainable, though it may be difficult to pursue or to ultimately grasp.

The two-marshmallow folks are also able to sense the unforeseen consequences of their current behaviors.

"If I don't stop texting my friends or commenting at these web sites I'll never get this homework done, and I'll get a bad grade. That will keep me out of graduate school, so I had better buckle down, now."

This seems perfectly normal to some of us. I earned five college degrees, including two very difficult ones, a Ph.D. and a Juris Doctor degree. I couldn't have done either if I hadn't resolved to turn off the TV and keep it in repose for years at a time.

Zimbardo speaks of his impoverished upbringing in New York. He learned the necessity to postpone gratification from a few influential teachers. If he had not, he wouldn't have amounted to very much.

It isn't enough to fashion and to maintain our long-term goals. We need short-term reinforcement thinking to assist.

Zig Ziglar, the motivational speaker wrote in his book, *See You At The Top*, that those that want to lose weight cannot do it all of a sudden.

We need reduce the same way we put the weight on: One bite at a time.

By repeatedly doing small things, we reach our largest goals. I discuss this at length in my bestselling audio seminar, "The Law of Large Numbers: How to Make Success Inevitable."

This means we need to do a lot of what we hope to master in order to become a master of whatever that is.

My daughter asked me yesterday whether she could publish her poetry. I told her by typing them and printing them off she has already "published," in the narrowest sense of the term.

If she wants others to publish her she needs to keep writing and her efforts will become more and more compelling. Then, others will be interested in putting her work in their publications.

We have become what we are through habits, which are repeated actions. And each of these repeated actions was the result of a thought.

The desire for instant gratification makes people crave instant success and celebrity. Sudden success only comes to very few.

More often, it comes extremely slowly before it is cashiered into a pile of money, fame, or even acceptance.

Jon Hamm, the handsome leading character in TV's "Mad Men," struggled for about 16 years in Hollywood before scoring the role that made his fame.

Actors such as Hamm become masters at the sort of thinking I'm advocating, here. They find outlets for their talent, accepting small roles here and there, while making the most of each that comes their way.

If they don't focus on the role they're playing now, or the one they're auditioning for, they'll fail to achieve success in it and fail in achieving personal gratification, as well.

They can't knock what they're doing while mistily pining over what they really want, fame, fortune, and wide acknowledgment of their talents. If they do, they won't be comfortable in their skin, this will show, and they'll repel opportunities that might come along.

They have to accept current circumstances without settling for them. Their minds must be on the present, but also be able to see to the horizon, and beyond.

Actors are uniquely equipped to do this because when they are in a scene they must function as the characters they are playing. Yet, simultaneously, they need to keep the audience or the camera angle in mind to technically comply with the demands that playing their character impose.

They're here as characters and here as themselves, at once. This is the same challenge as thinking about the now, being immersed in it, bit also fitting this moment into the big picture.

Zimbardo calls this "Living in multiple time zones." We are present oriented and future oriented, simultaneously.

Bruce Lee, the immortal martial artist and film and TV star, said "I do not fear the man that has made ten thousand different kicks; I fear the man that has made one kick ten thousand times."

As a martial artist I can tell you that when you begin to train, the novelty of being able to make all sorts of moves is very appealing. When you are first shown a kick or a hand strike or a parry, and you successfully do it, you get a rush of excitement.

And you feel you are better for having learned it.

But you haven't truly learned anything at that point. Your knowledge is mostly in your head. You saw an example of someone doing it, your trainer. You copied that.

And you then went on to the next move.

But can you replicate that kick or strike or parry on demand? Specifically, can you do it under actual fighting conditions, instantly and reflexively? Could you repeat that move in a nearly perfect or at least a sufficient manner to save your life or the life of a loved one?

Your abilities during the first several days, weeks, and months of your training are a mile wide but only an inch deep. Mastery of any given move or routine known as a *kata,* takes lots of repetition.

Your short-term thinking must be totally immersed in doing that one move, again and again. If you worry about it, "Gee I'm not getting this!" or "I'll never master this!" then you won't.

You'll be insufficiently in the present in your thinking by worrying about the future effectiveness of the move.

I've trained salespeople that fall into the same trap. They're so worried about whether a given technique will be effective that they sabotage its implementation.

Instead of making themselves repeat what they learned in training they improvise and never master any proven sequence that will achieve success and sales.

Like actors and martial artists, sellers need to commit to the present moment and do those things that will achieve long-term success without doubting whether these moves will lead to success.

Let go back to those marshmallow recipients. I would presume that at least some of those that grabbed he one item instead of waiting to get two, were worried that the experimenter was unreliable.

"Hey, what if I wait and I get no marshmallows?" at least a few must have wondered.

Better a marshmallow in hand than two in the bush, right?

In reality then, we need short term and long term thinking, but we also need at least a little faith that by doing "A," by doing a lot of "A," we'll achieve "B & C."

Without that belief that the future can add up to much more than the present, we'll probably keep reaching out for instant gratification, to our longer-term detriment.

23

Give Yourself A Good 20 Minutes
to Think!

People ask me, "When do you get your best ideas?"

We can start first by addressing *where* I get them, which is almost the same thing.

I do some of my best thinking at a Peet's coffee shop a few miles from my home. It's like a Starbuck's, but with an oaky vibe. Actually, there is a good amount of wood veneer near the cash registers, giving it a natural feel.

There aren't too many tables, but if you get there at the right time, you can snare one. Otherwise you're going to sit outside which isn't all bad.

This Peet's is about four miles from the ocean, and on most afternoons there is a breeze.

My home office is great, situated about fifty feet from a boat dock and channel. From my perch I can see water waving by, and it is a nice scene, as well.

But for generating my best new ideas, Peet's is the place.

I'm not trying to give them a special plug here, though their coffee is rich. I'm simply saying that is a great place for me to have some of my most creative new ideas.

And going there is a nice drive, people leave me to my thoughts and to my ever-present writing tablet. And when all is said and done, Peet's is part of my routine.

Where do you have your best thoughts, in the shower, when you're taking a walk or hike, or when you're driving?

It's important to know the answer to this question.

Thinking is far too valuable an activity to relegate to any old place. Environments need to be conducive to doing it.

For me, Peet's has the right mix of activity and peace, and the volume of voices and bean grinding seldom reaches a distracting pitch.

Back to the when question: I guess I am optimally productive there between 1:30 and 4:00.

Once, I had some extra time in the morning and the place was jammed. I squeezed in and started some work, but there were far to many new faces and sounds to deal with.

I had to leave, and I went back to my home office, which is a dream location compared to that crowded morning spot.

So, you have to pick your shots, but I would caution you about getting too picky. If you wait for the "perfect" time or place to think, you probably won't find it.

What I need is just a good twenty minutes . . .

This is almost a mantra for me and I share it with anyone who asks me how I create titles for my books, audios, videos, seminars, and coaching and consulting. When I can be at peace in a comfortable locale and let my mind wander for 20 minutes or so, my best thoughts jump into my mind.

Someone said that creativity is best accessed when the mind is at play.

My mind plays with what it perceives to be silly ideas, jokes, quirks and insoluble problems.

For example, I decided to offer communication training through a local college. I titled the program a "Communication Effectiveness Workshop."

I don't recall anyone signing up. What a drag! I wanted to teach in an area in which I had a lot of training, communication, but the world didn't want what I had to offer.

It so happened that I had a lot of business experience with telephone communication. I had been a collector for a financial company where my job was to make and take calls eight hours a day.

I also was in sales and sales management with Time Warner where using the phone was paramount to achieving success.

I don't know where I was but my mind was playing with the losing seminar title.

"So, nobody likes a Communication effectiveness program, then what would they like? And what do I know well enough to teach?"

Suddenly, he answer came to me: Why not Telephone Effectiveness?

I went back to the same college with that title and the class enrolled pretty well. I ran the class, successfully, and the next time I offered it, in the Midwest, we had 44 participants!

Suddenly, I had a winner that I would deliver hundreds of times through colleges and corporations around the world.

As you can see, being perfectly at peace may not be the only or the best path to creative thinking. Sometimes that path is paved with frustration, with anger, and with a desire to "show them!"

So people streamed into my telephone seminars, and I found one question kept popping up when I covered selling over the phone.

"Can you sell THIS by phone?" and they'd give me an example of a product or service. In every case, I replied, "Why not?"

But then I encountered some people that had a different opinion. They would challenge me: "You can't sell intangibles such as insurance, by phone, can you?"

Doing almost a seminar a day in different cities, these comments were frustrating me, and then a title for a book sprang into my mind:

You Can Sell Anything By Telephone!

Instantly, I knew it was going to be a bestseller. Not only that, it was going to be a poignant response to that incessant challenge I got.

Just one more example, dealing with books, if I may...

I was coaching three sports that my daughter was participating in: soccer, softball, and basketball.

As you can imagine, I was busy year-round. Soccer went well, and YMCA basketball, too.

But Little League Softball was a nightmare. The parents, even more than league officials, were a real handful.

I got the typical gripes about not playing certain kids more of the time. But tensions escalated and a parent challenged a decision of mine by angrily storming the field and facing off with me at close range when I was in the 3rd base coaching box.

You've heard the horror stories about out of control parents that start fights and worse. Well, I had a few of these creeps in the grandstands.

The softball season ended badly, but without any violence, thank goodness.

But I was frustrated and angry. I had put in a lot of time and effort into coaching and a few rotten apples really ruined the experience.

Ruminating about these rats, a book title sprang to mind, which I wrote and a publisher issued in record time:

101 Things Parents Should Know Before Volunteering To Coach Their Kids' Sports Teams.

I think it's a significant book that provides a true public service. Parents deserve to know what they're getting into, the pitfalls, perils as well as the pleasures of volunteer coaching.

Anyway, here again you can see that creativity can spring from disappointments and frustrations.

The key to thinking effectively about these setbacks is to ask, what good can come from them?

How can I turn a negative into a plus?

For me, it only takes a good 20 minutes to do.

It may take you more time or less, but that doesn't matter. Identify the conditions under which you think best, and then those conditions recur, make the most out of them!

24

Thinking Things Have To Be Perfect
Or That They Will Be

Aristotle, one of the deepest and best thinkers the Western humane inheritance has produced over the past 2,200 years said ours is a world of probabilities, and not certainties.

There is tremendous wisdom in that statement.

What does it mean, exactly, and how do I hope you'll benefit from knowing this and occasionally repeating it to yourself?

Let me tell you a story.

Steve went to law school, which is understandable because his father and grandfather also studied law. Grandfather more or less practiced law without a license.

Though he studied under a federal judge, and put in the required time to sit for the examination, he actually didn't want to take it. Back in his day, if you were a licensed attorney, you were forbidden from getting clients through advertising.

That stricture wasn't going to prevent him from getting clients or advertising for them. What he did was post the kinds of ads you see today in subways, on taxis, and on the sides and back of buses.

He did it not to advertise his services but as a way of soliciting cases that he would send to licensed attorneys. There was a loophole in the law that permitted him to do this and he took advantage of it until the state legislature passed a law making such a referral business illegal.

He was firmly told to take the bar exam or to stop practicing law, even if that wasn't what it did, strictly speaking.

His son, Steve's father was in law school while Steve's grandfather was doing business. Everybody knew everybody, and anybody who was anybody didn't like what Grandfather did, and they took it out on Steve's law student father.

That left a bitter taste so Steve's father decided to take a pass on sitting for the bar exam. Thus he didn't practice law, unofficially or officially. And this fact, that he went to law school but did not open an office became part of family lore.

Anyway, Steve went to law school, also, but after he was a successful businessman. He actually sat for the bar exam and passed it so he was licensed. By the time he reached that status the law had changed and law firms could advertise fairly freely.

Steve thought about practicing and even interviewed at some firms, but he was making more money in business than he could by practicing.

But he was torn. The law could be interesting, stimulating, and lucrative if you put in the time.

What Steve didn't like was what he heard professor after professor say. More or less they said you had better be perfect in practicing law, making zero errors. If you were less than 100% competent, your client could sue you.

After that, you might be disbarred, which was shameful. (Steve also had an uncle that was disbarred, much to the family's scorn.)

So Steve, though he felt he passed the bar with flying colors and really was sharp on the law, was intimidated. In his own business he could err from time to time and no one would notice or he could make good on his mistake.

He felt he faced practically zero risk of being sued in his enterprise, though in point of fact, he could be sued as can any business for practically anything at any time.

With the rise of the Internet, and reeling from The Great Recession, his regular business went through some dramatic changes. The net of this was that he closed it up.

Not knowing what to do to earn a living, he dismissed the idea of practicing law, though he kept his license up to date and continued his legal education, as required.

He took sales jobs that were far below his skills, simply to pay the bills. But he grew increasingly frustrated. Downward pressures were put on salespeople's incomes, so he didn't know what to do.

Out of the blue, a former client from his old business called him and asked for some legal advice, remembering Steve was an attorney. Resisting the urge to respond with his opinion, he nearly begged off of helping.

He was still intimidated based on that old set of warnings he heard in law school.

But he needed income, so he accepted his old client as a new law client.

Steve did a remarkably good job. His client was happy and he soon came back with another case for Steve to handle.

Steve felt great about himself and a weight had been lifted from him that he hadn't realized was there for many years. He realized he didn't have to be perfect to practice and to succeed.

Nobody's perfect. You do your best and hope for the best, and you learn from your mistakes.

This is something we all have to realize and take to heart.

Perfectionism is a major flaw in our thinking. It freezes us in certain cases. In others we're afraid to let go.

Artists who never feel a painting is finished keep painting long after the time they have a suitable product on the canvas in front of them.

Writers keep writing and rewriting that novel that never gets sent to a publisher.

Perfection, for many, leads to procrastination. For others who start projects, it leads to defeating oneself before finishing.

We simply cannot know in advance how anything is going to work out.

One company I worked with sent a dozen employees to my customer satisfaction seminar in Cincinnati, Ohio. They told an interesting story.

They had a customer who was so crabby, so time consuming, and emotionally taxing that the entire customer service team recommended to their company president that he "fire" that customer.

Give him his walking papers. Treat him as a persona non grata. Let a competitor suffer!

Simply, get rid of him.

The president heard this recommendation and said this, in reply.

"I will fire him if you'll do the following. First, treat him like a prince. Make him feel he is the best customer in the world. After 30 days, if he isn't markedly easier to get along with, we'll say goodbye; fair enough?"

Reluctantly, the staff agreed and they tried their best. This tale has a happy ending.

That ornery customer made a complete about-face. He turned into a fine person to do business with!

In fact, he ordered more products, increasing several fold the value of his account.

And he even became golfing buddies with the boss!

We don't know how anything or anyone is going to turn out. It was improbable that this customer was going to change his ways. But he did.

What hadn't been clear to the customer service reps was the tremendous influence they could exert in changing his behavior. They were all convinced he was perfectly imperfect!

There's no such thing, or person.

Mind your perfectionism. Don't impose impossible standards upon your own performance or that of others.

When you hear yourself doing otherwise, change that thought as quickly as you can.

You'll probably get better results than you hoped.

25

Is Scarcity Thinking Making You Poor?

For much of human history people have had to struggle just to survive.

In certain places on Earth, where desert is making watersheds disappear, along with the life it supports, this struggle is being repeated.

But in most of the developed world, starvation isn't nearly the stalker it once was. In fact, obesity, being over-fed is more of a danger to health, to well-being, and to survival.

Yet there is a perception in many folks that there isn't enough to go around.

There isn't enough money or opportunity to provide an adequate or a sufficient life.

This feeling of "There isn't enough for me" is more pronounced in an age when media outlets, operating in a 24-hour news cycle clamor for the largest possible audience in a time when audience size is shrinking because of the proliferation of communication channels spawned by the Internet.

To achieve audience ratings broadcasters exaggerate the news, wresting from many events the worst-case scenarios that can emerge. These gloom and doom characterizations keep people riveted to certain channels that promote hysterical reactions.

Viewers, listeners, and readers that are already highly disposed to use distorted thinking react obsessively and are put into a state of "irrational anxiety," one of the symptoms of neurosis, a mental disorder.

In the depths of an economic recession, people are told, repeatedly, that their prospects of finding employment are bleak. In truth, this belief, that it is almost impossible to get work if the economy overall is shrinking, is the greatest obstacle to finding it.

Let's look back to the great recession that began back in 2008-2009. The nation's unemployment rate was pegged at about 10.5 percent.

News outlets would note this figure, but they would go on to observe that the official rate is always not the entire story.

It doesn't factor in the greater impacts upon young and older persons who find it harder to get work in any circumstance, so they suffer an even greater adverse impact from a shrinking economy.

Plus outlets would say that the official rate is always unrepresentative because many folks have simply given up looking for work driven by the perception that it is fruitless to try to find employment. National unemployment rates leave these hapless and hopeless folks out of the equation.

Not to understate the very real pain that privation promotes, let's look at the other side of the story, as a famous broadcaster was fond of saying.

If the official employment rate is 10.5% then this means the great majority of people in the labor market, 89.5% ARE working. Policy makers that say even 10.5% official employment is too high, that we should strive for full employment, have my endorsement along with that of many economists.

Still, there is a lot of good news, or at least an absence of bad news for those that are being paid to toil.

Your outlook will depend on what you choose to focus on.

Moreover, in the worst of recent economic woes, there were still companies that had open positions that were advertised yet remained unfilled.

The labor market is notoriously inefficient. Job seekers and job providers don't come together in a quick, cost-effective manner. Far from it, in good and bad times there are opportunities where employers are saying, "If only I had the right candidate for the job, I could expand my business."

Robert Schuller, whose family suffered in the Dust Bowl during the Great Depression, noted that most of us don't have a money problem.

We have an idea problem.

Insufficient funding is a symptom. The disease is that we are bankrupt when it comes to our inventory of potential solutions.

One thing we must challenge is the thought that there is scarcity "out there," beyond the confines of our minds. Most of our troubles are rooted in the thought that times are tough all over and we can't do anything about them.

One of America's Big-3 carmakers was on strike, and in a particular community where there was a large facility where people talked incessantly about hard times, sharing their fears of the future.

But there was a real estate salesperson that was thrilled, according to motivational speaker and writer Zig Ziglar. The Realtor noticed that some people found the strike gave them a chance to take more time to shop for homes, and they took advantage of this fact.

Also, because of the widespread worry regarding the strike, home prices had softened. Confident that the carmaker would settle its differences with the union, some folks were harvesting the bargain properties that were available.

The economist, Schumpeter, called this process "creative destruction." In this context, it says one person's woe creates another person's opportunity.

The Internet savaged many brick and mortar bookstores with the rapid rise of companies such as Amazon. While many chains and independent booksellers suffered, some thrived by morphing into cafés and lecture venues.

Other stores, that had tens of thousands of used books on site, such as Powell's, suddenly had through the Internet millions of potential international clients to whom these books could be sold.

This phenomenon is reminiscent of one of the laws of thermodynamics that says matter is never completely destroyed, but it is transformed.

Job losses in certain sectors are often translated into job gains in others.

And this summons the famous opening passage of Dickens' *Tale of Two Cities*, when he writes, "It was the best of times and it was the worst of times."

It's always the best of times and the worst of times, depending on who you are and what you choose to believe.

Pioneering producer Mike Todd once said, "I've never been poor, but I have been broke."

Being broke is not having funds at a given time. It is temporary. Being poor is a state of mind that is far worse.

You can be broke, but be rich in other things, such as good health, great friendships, and in having a wonderfully supportive and loving family.

I remember growing up and my dad would tell me from time to time that "Money is tight" and as a result fewer firms were purchasing advertising from him.

Frankly, I had no idea what this meant, tight money.

Later, I'd study the banking system and the Federal Reserve, which decides how much money to circulate in the economy. I found there is support for the concept of money being tight or loose, or more accurately being like water in a spigot.

Sometimes it trickles or it can gush forth, depending on who is controlling the faucet.

When it flows freely, the economy tends to expand, and when the flow is restricted, the economy tends to shrink.

But these are generalizations.

Personally, I have made larger sums in tough times than I have made in lush times. Partly, this is the result of the fact that companies look to outside consultants to help them when sales are slipping.

In good times, they don't have sales problems nearly as much, but their focus shifts to customer service, to satisfying and holding onto the customers they already have.

Thus, I have different packages I feature at different times in the economic cycle.

Being able to adapt quickly to the changing needs of employers and to the requirements of various stages of the economy is essential to succeeding, irrespective of the external circumstances we face.

But above all, this is a thinking challenge. We need to ask ourselves, what do I have to do right now to benefit?

This question presupposes that there is a fruitful course of action to follow, that there are always options, some good and some better, that we can uncover and pursue.

As long as some people are prospering, so can we, providing we use our thinking power to conceptualize abundance instead of scarcity.

26

How To Avoid
Ineffective Decision Making

One of the traps people fall into is using the wrong thinking when making decisions.

Typically, most people do one or more of the following things.

They react emotionally when circumstances seem to call for a decision.

Sometimes, they freeze up, worried that they'll make an imprudent choice. This leads to procrastination, to self-derision, and to allowing the fates and other people to influence outcomes.

Pausing before choosing a course of action is often wise, providing you're going to use the analytical part of your brain to calculate the risks and rewards posed by a situation.

In fact, people that try to take advantage of us often do so by rushing us. They could be sellers that hope we'll make a snap-decision in their favor.

There is a word that is synonymous with being conned by the unscrupulous. It is being "hustled." At the heart of a hustle is being rushed.

So, again, taking some time to think over any proposition is wise. And you want to be on your guard against those that urge you to act without reflecting.

To guard against being ripped-off or making an error of judgment, some people adopt a "24-hour rule" or insist on being given time to "sleep on" any significant decision they're being asked to make.

Few situations are so urgent that they require a reflexive response instead of a reflective one.

By the way, there are two kinds of urgency that you'll encounter, especially in contexts where you are being asked to purchase.

The first type is "Internal urgency." This is man-made.

For example, someone may make a proposal to you and insist that your affirmative response be forthcoming by Friday morning; otherwise the offer will expire.

Apart from the fact that your counterpart in the transaction would like to settle matters by that time, there is no necessary correlation between the underlying offer and your promptest reply.

Friday could be extended to Monday, or to a week or month hence, if you ask for an extension.

The second type is "External urgency." This is an outside force beyond the control of the other person.

If your counterpart says you must buy on Friday morning or before because his inventory is running out and he is facing a 25% price increase after that from his wholesaler, then this is an external force that is creating urgency.

There is a greater claim to authenticity to external urgency than to internal. Still, you could be hearing a story that is simply another maneuver to get you off the fence to make a hasty decision.

Peter F. Drucker conducted a class that I attended on the Effective Decision. One of the important takeaways from it is this crucial threshold question:

Must a decision be made?

This is actually a decision, in itself, determining if you simply must decide.

Possibly, as Governor Jerry Brown of California once said, "Not doing something can be the highest form of action."

Although people are excoriated for having endless meetings that seem to accomplish little, there is wisdom sometimes in a group deciding to "Table a matter until a future date."

This is so because making a decision of any kind has consequences, some of which are intended, and others that are unintended.

For example, I may encourage a client to sign a consulting contract that provides certain guarantees. If they don't get the specified results I am pursuing for them, they can pay less or be released from a responsibility to pay, altogether.

I provide guarantees for the very purpose of bypassing the tendency firms have of tabling my proposals or not approving them because they entail some risks.

I am short-circuiting the decision avoidance process. If I can eliminate most if not all risks, and the rewards seem likely, there are few remaining reasons to not move forward.

This can be good for all parties, presuming I'm good at what I do and what I do, works. They save time and effort in making a decision, and I spend less time offering assurances, testimonials and responding to what-if questions.

However, even if I offer what some refer to as a money-back guarantee, or a you-don't-pay-if-you-aren't-satisfied offer, if accepted, there are still some costs that clients will incur.

There are coordination costs, meaning I need to arrange details of delivering my services with people on the staff. Employees need to be shepherded into training rooms, and their time away from their regular duties is also a cost.

And if my failure to achieve results is conspicuous, this may have ramifications for those that hired me in the first place, even if they didn't have to pay me a dime, out of pocket.

If I "poison the well" so to speak as a consultant by doing an inadequate job, it may be harder for the next consultant that comes along to successfully engage that company, to his or her detriment as well as to the company's.

These are some of the unintended consequences of a decision. I'm saying, even if there seem to me no costs whatsoever, there are always costs, nonetheless.

Typically, decisions are made to solve problems. If there isn't a definable problem, there is often no need for a solution.

The problem should be definable, pressing, and meaningful.

Still, if the problem exists, but there is no known or readily available or affordable solution, then a decision to act is not possible or really beneficial.

Some years ago, a scientist working for 3M Company found that a glue that he fabricated failed to create a permanent bond between objects. In that sense, it was a failure, with no known application.

But this scientist asked an unusual question, something like this: What would be a practical use of an adhesive that created a temporary bond, but not a permanent one?

The answer was Post-It Notes®. You're probably familiar with them.

These are colorful slips of paper that come in pads that can be used to put notes on surfaces such as desks and refrigerators. Typically, they're used as reminders and they take the place of using a piece of paper and some tape. They save time and money, and they became a hit and a big profit-maker for 3M.

I present this case for the purpose of saying that decisions don't always take a problem-to-solution path. Sometimes, they do the reverse, working from a solution back to identifying a problem.

Much of science proceeds from such "happy accidents." Penicillin, a life-saving drug, was discovered this way.

A proven way to guard against making ineffective decisions is to involve more people in the process.

The Japanese became known for consensual decision making. When they were about to adopt a technique or a technology they would involve practically everyone who would be touched by that innovation to provide input as to its impacts, effectiveness, ease of use, and deleterious effects.

Before adoption, there had to be agreement among all of these stakeholders, and this consumed quite a lot of time.

To the Western way of decision-making, this seemed grossly inefficient. Occidentals were used to one or very few people at the top of a firm deciding on behalf of those that would implement the new processes.

The Japanese supported their approach by acknowledging that it did take more time to formulate decisions, but they were better ones. Flaws in proposed processes and technologies were more likely to surface earlier in the adoption cycle, incurring fewer costs.

And implementation was swift and easy because so many implementers had been consulted before the decision to adopt was made.

Another question to ask that can aid you in making better decisions is this one:

How viable, easy or expensive is it to reverse this decision?

Once the horse is out of the barn can you retrieve him, or is he lost forever?

The decision to tool up an assembly line to mass-produce a car or truck is exceedingly costly. But a decision to make a working prototype, and then to test its appeal at car shows, is a relatively minor cost, with huge advantages. Prototyping provides the choice to later go into full production, to adapt only some of the prototype's features into existing models, or to abandon the project, altogether.

To summarize, ask if a decision is really necessary. Beware of the temptation to make hasty decisions, especially if other parties in their self-interests are goading you to do so.

Use the problem-solution format for making a decision. Is there a problem that is so pressing and significant that it needs to be solved? Do solutions exist, and are they viable and cost-effective?

What are the foreseeable and unforeseen consequences of making and implementing the decision? If you cannot bracket or anticipate all of the costs, can you at least contain them by offering or insisting on receiving guarantees?

And consider using more of a Japanese model of decision-making that involves more people and takes more time on the front end, while saving time at the implementation stage.

These considerations should clarify your thinking and help you to make better decisions.

27

Thinking Out Loud:
What Are You Telling Yourself?

Author and enlightenment guru Eckhart Tolle tells a story in of one of his books.

He spotted a woman on the street that was engaged in a lively conversation, with herself. She was quite animated as she walked by, waving her hands, cocking her head, speeding and slowing her pace, for emphasis.

He thought she was a bit odd. But he had an overwhelming urge to follow her.

As she continued her frenzied walk, taking turn after turn, crossing various streets, Tolle felt an odd sense of déjà vu.

Then, his weird feeling of familiarity was confirmed.

She entered the same building where he worked!

"Could this strange lady be a colleague?" he wondered.

Stepping into the rest room he washed his hands and saw himself the mirror. He was muttering to himself, babbling about this quirky person in the same way she was babbling about something or some other non-present being.

This shocked him. Was he as daffy as he thought she was?

After all, he was doing the same things, muttering, carrying on.

I share this tale with you to point out that we all talk to ourselves. Some of us move our lips, making it easy for witnesses to think us strange.

But self-talk is almost ceaseless. We might label it as just a more slightly audible mode of thinking.

The real challenge is to become aware of what we are telling ourselves about ourselves and about other people and the world around us.

Often, if you tune into these self-chats you'll find thoughts are repeatedly negative or dysfunctional. They actually disable us and impede our progress toward positive goals.

And as they are repeated in the echo chambers of our minds, they become stronger and more convincing.

What are some of the thoughts we think? What do we incessantly say to ourselves?

Let's start with just 21 examples:

If I look at food, I gain weight!
I don't have a creative bone in my body!
I'm unlucky!
I just can't win!
Nobody likes me!
Nothing good lasts!

People really upset me!
I'm always broke!
Everyone in my family is a hard drinker!
I am so dumb!
I'll never quit smoking!
I'm just not employee material!
The other shoe will drop; just wait!
People always take advantage of me!
I'm bad at making friends!
I attract trouble like a magnet!
There are no jobs out there!
I'm not qualified enough to be a dishwasher!
There's no use in trying!
If I don't get enough sleep I'm no good to anybody!
Another Monday!

How many of these negative thoughts have you repeated to yourself? And what is the impact on your behavior when you take any of these notions to heart?

These thoughts don't lead us to happiness.

If I were to summarize them under a heading I would probably say they paint us as victims.

Almost every one says, "I have no control over effectiveness," and "This is the way I am; I simply can't change."

As I have mentioned, when we pick up on the fact we're telling ourselves something that isn't helping our cause, we need to stop at that moment of perception.

"Hey, that's a negative thought I'm fostering!" we should note.

"What did I just tell myself, again? *I'm unlucky?* Why do I think I'm unlucky?"

At that point a cascade of memories will pass by you. Your mind will summon a parade of episodes that will support this belief.

But you can't stop there because you'll only confirm the apparent "fact" that you only have one kind of luck, bad luck.

This is normal because perception is selective. If we look to the past to prove practically any proposition, we can find support for it. We're going to use this proclivity to prove the opposite to be true.

"What contrary evidence do I have to support the fact that I'm VERY lucky?" we should ask.

By the way, we all are exceedingly lucky; let me point this out from the get-go.

We're lucky to be alive! Do you know how many close calls with death or disability our ancestors had before they spawned our parents? How many lions, tigers, bears, and diseases did they have to outrun or outlast?

Just being present to consider your luck or lack of luck is very lucky! What a luxury it is that we're even here.

The problem with thinking you are unlucky is that you will come to expect bad things to happen. And if this is your belief, even potentially positive events will be misconstrued as being bad.

The same can be said about the list of 21 negative self-statements. Each one sets-up traps in the future that will trip us up.

If we say, "I'm just not employee material!" we are setting ourselves up to become alienated from every job we're going to have.

These statements become imperatives. All of them say I am a certain way and this is going to repeat itself.

We have to break these patterns of thought.

For one thing, we need to endorse a major premise: we have more control than we think over the outcomes we achieve.

People don't "drive us nuts." We're the ones in the driver's seat.

To get to this idea we may need to endorse a bridge-belief.

For example, we need to tell ourselves, "Just because something once strongly affected my life doesn't not mean it must always affect it."

So, while there may be some evidence to support the idea that many people have been hard drinkers in our family, this doesn't mean we MUST be one, as well.

History, in other words, is not destiny. And this is especially true about other people's histories, irrespective of whether they are related to us.

But back to us, we go. Just because we have been taken advantage of by some people doesn't necessarily mean this pattern, if it existed, must persist into the future.

We can change our outcomes, but first we must change our negative self-talk.

Substitute positive alternatives.

Replace the "I'm so dumb!" self-statement by entertaining the idea that "I'm very smart!"

Write down your strengths, all of them.

You'll be impressed with how many you have.

If this is hard, then start with your "21" list of presumed weaknesses and shortcomings. Then dispute each one, summoning evidence to prove its opposite.

If you tell yourself, "I can't win!" or "I'm a loser!" then recap all of your victories, no matter how long ago they occurred.

I can do some pretty accurate mathematical calculations in my mind when I want to.

But to do this I've had to overcome the belief that I was bad at math.

Where did that thought come from? I had no patience for my math classes in high school, and my teachers were not what you might call, inspired.

So, my grades suffered, and because of these experiences I came to doubt my innate math aptitude.

But I decided to challenge this assumption. I asked, "Is there evidence to support the idea that I'm really good at math?"

There was!

In primary school I earned excellent grades!

In fact, there was more support for my being good at math than there was that I was bad at it.

So I put this to the test by deliberately activating that part of my mind that can do mental calculations. Through repeated successes, I now have much more confidence in this capability.

And I enjoy myself much more and my career is more rewarding.

So, to summarize, we're always going to talk to ourselves. Start tuning in. Is what you're saying positive? If not, note specifically what you're hypnotizing yourself into believing.

Prove the opposite.

You'll not only straighten out your thinking, but you'll probably become much more successful and happier.

28

Black Swans & Over-Generalizing

Every now and then, an event occurs that changes outlooks, instantly.

The attacks on Pearl Harbor and 9-11 come to mind. These are cleavage points, where there seems to have been one kind of strategic thinking before them and an entirely different mindset afterwards.

These are called Black Swan events.

According to Wikipedia:

"The Black Swan theory of events is a metaphor that describes an event that comes as a surprise, has a major effect, and is often inappropriately rationalized after the fact with the benefit of hindsight."

Pearl Harbor disputed the idea that Honolulu was safely beyond the reach of Japanese military aviation. More broadly, it violated the idea that battles were set pieces, like chessmen lined-up in neat rows waiting for a battle to get underway.

"Meeting on the field of battle" was a long tradition. Militaries faced off at certain locations and everyone knew a large battle was about to ensue.

But the "sneak attack" on Pearl Harbor, as it was repeatedly referred to for decades, seemed particularly malevolent, not only in the damage it reaped, but in its element of surprise.

Surprise is an essential ingredient of the Black Swan. It catches us off guard. From the outset whatever occurs seems impossible, not only improbable.

Wikipedia explains:

"When the phrase was coined, the black swan was presumed not to exist. The importance of the metaphor lies in its analogy to the fragility of any system of thought. A set of conclusions is potentially undone once any of its fundamental postulates is disproved. In this case, the observation of a single black swan would be the undoing of the logic of any system of thought, as well as any reasoning that followed from that underlying logic."

Author Nassim Nicholas Taleb explains in his book, *The Black Swan* that there are three aspects to this phenomenon:

"First, it is an outlier, as it lies outside the realm of regular expectations, because nothing in the past can convincingly point to its possibility. Second, it carries an extreme 'impact'. Third, in spite of its outlier status, human nature makes us concoct explanations for

its occurrence after the fact, making it explainable and
predictable.

"A small number of Black Swans explains almost everything in our world, from the success of ideas and religions, to the dynamics of historical events, to elements of our own personal lives."

In the case of a Pearl Harbor or a 9-11, one's illusion of safety is shattered. Suddenly, nothing seems as if it will be the same.

I was on business in Florida when 9-11 occurred. Planes were grounded for a few days. I was booked on the first flight from Miami to Los Angeles after the grounding was lifted.

Airport security scrutiny was intense. We boarded, were ushered off the plane and re-boarded.

Just before takeoff I was dozing to sleep when the flight attendant woke me up. In so many words she told me I was expected to do my part to thwart any attack on the flight deck because I was seated only a few rows away from it.

Flying would never be the same.

Because I was a consultant who flew weekly, my business was almost made unrecognizable after 9-11. I had to factor in cancelled flights, long and costly delays, and a huge amount of added stress.

Companies were hesitant to send their people to seminars in various parts of the country, which meant less exposure for my ideas and for me, and this curtailed the amount of business I earned.

9-11 created an incubator for another Black Swan: The Internet.

Partly because travel became more difficult and expensive, the net and email provided a platform for sharing information that substituted for face-to-face meetings.

Black Swans only look predictable in retrospect. No one thought planes would be used as guided missiles to take down some of the largest buildings in New York, and to simultaneously attack the Pentagon, in Washington.

But instantly, what was impossible suddenly seemed likely and even inevitable. People could see warning signals, but only afterwards, which of course is no warning, at all.

This is where our thinking betrays us. We move from "impossible" to "inevitable" in our generalizations. And both perceptions are distorted.

What we can safely say is there will be Black Swans.

In 2008-2009 the American stock exchanges crashed. Shares in the best companies plummeted and we entered a severe recession that many called a depression.

Warren Buffett, who owned shares in the international giant, General Electric, decided to pump billions of additional dollars into the company. The stock had fallen from a high around $28 to about $5.

He explained that at $5 he was paying less than what one of GE's light bulb products cost.

Today, this story confirms Buffett's savvy. But there was no clear sign matters were going to improve.

Indeed, I had purchased GE stock starting at $27 a share all the way down to $18, but I had to sell at a steep loss. Unlike Buffett, I envisioned no recovery on the horizon.

He saw the stock market collapse and the banking crisis as a Black Swan, a one-time surprise that few predicted.

And he then scoped out the bargains and opportunities while nearly everyone else was waiting for the next shoe to drop.

But in terms of investment opportunities, that shoe may have dangled precariously, but it never fell.

I said Black Swan events do occur. How, if at all, can we prepare for them?

We can expect them but we cannot fully prepare. We insure, for example, against floods and earthquakes, fires and car accidents. These are known risks that repeat themselves and actuaries can plot their likelihood and impacts.

But against unknown risks there are no insurance policies.

Black Swans tell us things will never be the same, and technically speaking, this is true.

But that GE stock did recover to its former high price only four or five years after it bottomed.

There has not been another 9-11, executed the way it was, and this is largely because of stepped-up security procedures.

But there have been other attacks, and there will be more.

Peter F. Drucker was fond of saying no one can predict the future. The best we can do is to notice what others haven't detected and to act on the opportunities and challenges that have evaded perception.

This means, in spite of Black Swans, French journalist Alphonse Carr, writing in the 1800's, was also correct in noting, "The more things change, the more they stay the same."

But don't get too complacent.

29

Do No Harm

We get in our own way, causing ourselves no end of troubles, disappointments and setbacks.

Stinking Thinking is at the root of many foibles.

I recall taking an LA to Houston flight on a weekly basis over the course of two years. Flight crews got to know me.

On one occasion I was seated next to the CEO of the carrier. He was having a lot of problems with his labor unions, and it was widely reported that he was unpopular.

I had no idea how deeply the negative feelings ran until after I chatted with him during that flight.

I was walking to baggage claim and a cadre of flight attendants flanked me and asked, "How could you talk with that man?"

I was flummoxed.

Not only were they bad-mouthing the boss, they were doing it to one of their frequent flyers.

I just mumbled something incoherent and we all went on our way.

Their behavior was evidence that the CEO had stayed at his post beyond the point at which he could be effective. If his workers were willing to sabotage their company as they seemed ready to do, then he should have been attuned to this sorry state and have extricated himself.

Knowing when were are in over our heads, or that we have reached a level of inertness is a sign of an aware thinker.

There needs to be an auto-correcting feature in our thinking that goes off like an alarm in the cockpit. If we keep going in the direction we're heading, catastrophe could result.

He didn't have that, or in his grandiosity, he refused to acknowledge that he was part of the problem and not part of the solution.

The Hippocratic oath that physicians have been taking since ancient Greece does not say they have to help every person that comes to them, a common misperception.

It says: Do No Harm.

I believe this is an essential oath all of us should take. When we become aware of the possibility that we're not in the right frame of mind to interact with others, or that we are temporarily incapable of doing so without causing or aggravating harm, we should stop in our tracks.

Yesterday, I was in this exact mental space.

A customer returned to do business with me. I had served him before, but he wasted a lot of my time and then I found he was doing some business with a competitor.

In business there are few things as frustrating as investing a lot of time without getting a suitable return on that investment. This fellow's business was never lucrative.

Indeed, I would say I may have broken even or lost a few dollars when all was said and done.

Now that he was returning for more, I was conflicted.

Should I serve him again and watch helplessly as he uses me only to gain leverage, to wrest concessions from one of my competitors?

Fool me once, shame on you. Fool me twice, shame on me, correct?

Feeling as I did, should I tell him to take his business elsewhere? Or should I squelch my concerns and try to proceed as if nothing negative had occurred?

Unfortunately, he and I were not the only participants in the transaction. We had partners and other beneficiaries of our conduct.

If I acted badly, or even if I unconsciously gave less than my all to the transaction than it required, others could suffer. Yet if I extricated myself, substituting an associate for my presence, this would take time and effort, subjecting me to a loss of time equal to or greater than what I feared I'd lose by interacting, directly.

This is one of the 80/20 situations you may have heard of. To put it succinctly, the 80/20 "rule" says 80% of your income will come from 20% of your clients.

But 20% of your clients will "waste" or consume 80% of your time.

So, as a businessperson or even as an employee, if you can distinguish the most and least profitable clients you can allocate your time, accordingly.

In other words, try to spend 80% of your efforts on the 20% who give you the most income.

Management guru Peter F. Drucker put it this way: "Feed the winners and starve the losers."

This runs contrary to a sense of fairness, however. In an ideal world, we would treat all clients equally.

A restaurant would be as diligent in serving and re-filling a poor student's coffee cup as it would with a banquet table of big spenders.

And who knows?

That student could turn out to be someone who will profitably patronize your place in the decades to come.

Doing-good and doing-well could be linked if we look at these decisions in a larger timeframe.

That returning client of mine might succeed wildly at some point and realize that I've been on tap for him and I showed loyalty back in the day.

What did I do? Did I take his business or refuse?

I went ahead and worked with him, in spite of my reservations. And I tried to show patience, perhaps even more that I would have done with an account his size, because I was aware of my bias.

He did waste my time, not completely, but enough to rankle me.

I showed restraint and instead of taking him to task, saying something like, "Never darken my doorstep, again!" I made an effort to do no harm.

Still, I wasn't perfectly opaque. Something seethed through in one of my emails, I believe.

I regret that.

It's part of the Oath of Hippocrates, as well. But in this case, it is embodied in the common law.

If we're going to undertake a duty toward someone, we should exercise that duty reasonably well.

If you decide to help a frail person to cross the street you cannot stop halfway, leaving her to get to the other side.

If you were to do this, you would be doing more harm than good.

Every thought and deed has its consequences. Some are intended. Others are unintended.

In the example I provided of deciding to work again with my client, I put myself in a situation where I could be rewarded or punished.

I also signed-on in a sense for the afterthoughts that would occur to me as a consequence of the choice I had made.

If I shooed him away, forcing him to find another source to work with, I would have castigated myself for turning down some potential business.

Having decades of business experience under my belt I know that it is all too easy to swing like a pendulum from elation and arrogance to despair and desperation, based on the boom and bust cycles of the economy or one's bank account balances.

To this day, I recall being 18 and ordering a juicy double burger at my favorite restaurant and leaving most of it, uneaten, because I was feeling under the weather.

I remember saying no to six-figure consulting contracts because they were far less than the amount I initially asked for.

One of my habits, in other words, it to regret giving up goodies that were in the palm of my hand because I was in the wrong mood to embrace them, or I thought a handful wasn't enough, that I was being slighted.

But if I said yes and my client wasted my time and I could have been productively focused elsewhere, I'd also have regrets.

Psychologists call these possible torments aspects of post-decisional dissonance.

And they say having these thoughts is inevitable, to an extent. We'll always be haunted by un-chosen alternatives.

For now, it is wise enough to do no harm. Don't put yourself in situations where you won't give your best or even if you do you'll be inclined to second-guess your decision, wasting even more of your time, energy, and focus.

30

Don't Drink The Kool-Aid

One of the most gratifying aspects of being human is we can relate to other people.

This happens in families, friendships, on the job, as soccer moms and dads, and as fellow citizens.

Bonding based on perceived similarities comes naturally.

Early on in our lives, we are taught how to recognize other members of our tribes, to share indicia of these connections though words and gestures, clothing and commitments.

Assimilation and contrast are psychological devices that we hew to, unconsciously.

We tend to see those that we sense are like us as even more like us than they are.

And we tend to contrast even more than would be accurate those that seem different.

This drive to identify with others and to create affiliations is normal and even desirable. Kids sign-up for sports teams and bond with their teammates while trying to defeat their rivals.

Later, they'll join organizations that they'll champion sometimes in direct opposition to competing corporations.

Loyalty to their respective entities will promote teamwork, sacrifice, and will likely boost their productivity, profits, and incomes.

But taking sides has a dark aspect.

High school cliques are famous for rewarding cool kids while marginalizing everyone else. When this behavior goes to extremes, hazing and violence enforce in-group and out-group norms and relations.

Extremism is a common perversion of identification, of the desire to belong, to feel the comfort and safety of affiliations.

Indeed, according to philosopher Kenneth Burke, wars are a predictable, though lamentable "Disease of cooperation." It takes many acts of cooperation within our group and even with an adversarial group to host a war and abide by the "rules of engagement."

At the base of wars is an over-identification of the in-group with a concomitant alienation from and vilification of the evil, other.

It's very difficult to kill or to severely injure someone unless you can feel convinced that he is not-you.

Put another way, if we believe someone else is–us, that there is no place where we end and he begins, there is no daylight between us, how can we ever bring ourselves to harm him?

Kenneth Burke says the fact that we are like everyone in some ways and unlike them in others, is "The classical invitation to communicate."

We must cross a divide to gain support for our beliefs and initiatives.

If we were completely different we couldn't communicate. If we were all the same, we wouldn't need to communicate.

Burke says it is this "dancing of opposites," being like and yet unlike others that requires us to keep communicating.

Yet this dance is far from perfect and too often, the music threatens to stop.

This is when diplomacy or communication feels impossible because differences are so exaggerated that there seems to be no common ground.

Nations close their embassies in other lands, recalling their ambassadors. Parents and children refuse to reach out to each other over decades of time.

Teachers ignore certain students. People stop listening to each other and they hurl expletives and accusations like Molotov cocktails.

At the heart of conflicts we typically find several core issues. One of the most profound is fear.

Fear comes from our drive to survive. Typically, we believe there are scarce resources and if someone else gets them it will be at our expense.

Only in the most rare of circumstances is this true today, especially in developed nations. And in the most deprived countries, starvation is exceedingly rare.

Building on the dire predictions of Malthus before him, Dr. Paul Ehrlich made an argument in the 1960's and 1970's that the world was facing imminent, mass starvation and inevitable wars as a result.

His book, *The Population Bomb*, foretold this doom, and it became a bestseller. Ehrlich became a late night TV staple, and a guru. Millions of people across the world changed their procreation plans because Ehrlich had so forcefully argued that it was anti-social to consign future offspring to a hellish future.

What made him seem so genuinely prophetic was his embrace of mathematics and science. He cited trends, shared startling statistics, and carried convincing charts.

Today, we have a planet that fosters about two billion more people than it did during Ehrlich's heyday. Yet there is less famine and hunger than there was when he roamed the airwaves.

What happened, and how could he be so wrong?

In a word, *technology* happened.

The planet's ability to get a higher yield from planted crops, and especially from rice, a world staple, increased significantly. Our production of food outpaced our consumption of it.

This caught Ehrlich and his devotees by surprise.

But his folly is emblematic of the consequences of extreme thinking and especially of generalizing to extremes from the data in front of us.

Seldom are things so bad or so good as they appear, and especially as they are made out to be by people that have an vested interest in exploiting their exaggeration.

While Ehrlich was cursing the darkness scientists were at work to illuminate the pathway from predicted scarcity to abundance.

Reportedly, Ehrlich in recent years has been queried about his famous flop, about the conclusion that never came true about massive starvation.

His response is typical of so many end-of-the-worlders that sell their visions of doom and gloom.

He said the respite from starvation is only temporary. Given time, starvation will afflict humanity.

This is akin to those hellfire and brimstone preachers that say the end is nigh. Some even set a specific date for Armageddon, and when that date uneventfully passes, they say the wrathful mover of the universe is merciful, as well.

But don't get too cozy, they warn. Soon, there will be new date announced, another date with destiny.

Ehrlich's seems like a quaint and rare goof, now, decades later. But there is a brand new book penned by a very prestigious economist from Northwestern University who is touting a similar, if slightly less dramatic thesis.

He says the great period of innovation in society has passed. It occurred from 1870 until around 1960. Since that time, nothing as dramatically life changing as indoor plumbing, electric lighting, the automobile, and a few other items, have been as significant.

From this point, we may seem tiny enhancements, but don't look for major breakthroughs.

He has his detractors, of course. They say the Internet is hugely influential and new, and look for more discoveries in genetics and nanotechnologies. Some say there will be breakthroughs not in manufacturing, as such, but in better and more efficient distribution.

This concept, that humanity is limited, that we are in or facing scarcity, be it of food or technologies, is an unsupportable generalization.

Arguing for the limits of humanity has always been foolish because we are surprisingly creative, adaptable, and durable.

Charles H. Duell was the Commissioner of US patent office in 1899. Mr. Deull's most famous utterance was that "Everything that can be invented has been invented."

If anyone was in a position to make such a blanket generalization, it was Mr. Duell. After all, across his desk came reams of new inventions, each of which was arguably distinctive.

But he could see they were mostly derivative, with minor distinctions.

Yet his quote is wildly bogus and off the mark.

Avoid extremes in your thinking and by any means avoid the zealots who proclaim to have the truth and the only truth.

These are the hucksters and mindbenders that would have you raise a glass to doom.

Well, as Jim Jones' followers would probably say, if they could tell tales, is "Don't drink the Kool-Aid!"

31

Can You Count to Ten?

For every rule, there are exceptions; we know this.

Most of us have been taught as children to "Think before you speak," to not fly off the handle, and to calmly assess situations before we act.

And you would expect me to advise caution, as well, considering I am authoring this project with an eye toward eliminating or at least reducing our mental mistakes.

Not thinking enough before we act seems to be a very common mental error.

I was putting together a relationship with a well-known company. I had cultivated its CEO over many months and he brought me in to have a meeting with his team.

A few of them were threatened by my presence, including a lawyer. As he was showing me out, he barked, "We're going to need a non-compete agreement!"

Reflexively and defensively, my inner-lawyer shot back, "So will I!"

Today, I realize that quick response didn't win his support, as you can imagine. He was baiting me, and I swallowed it.

On a deeper level, if that group was the one I had to interact with, and this seemed to be the case, then we probably didn't have a genuine meeting of the minds to begin with, and this signaled trouble.

My defensiveness wasn't unreasonable; it had a foundation. As the old joke says, just because you are paranoid this doesn't mean they are not out to get you!

Daniel Kahneman is a Nobel Prize winning behavioral economist and author of an important book, *Thinking: Fast & Slow.*

As the title says, there are two thinking speeds.

Our Fast thinking is the ability to sense a threat or a reward and to respond in a lightening quick manner. You're hunting near a pond and you sense the presence of a pouncing puma.

Instantly, you need to assess your situation, which calls for running away, fighting it out, or staying perfectly still.

Your options are operating on Fast thinking.

Selecting the right one will determine whether you live or die. You have no time to calmly deliberate.

But what if you're taking a multiple-choice exam. Time to answer every question is limited.

Three choices are offered. "A" is correct. "B" could also be correct. And "C" says Both A & B are correct.

You read "A" first and you know that is right and you are about to check it off. Your Fast thinking is at work, and it seeks instant satisfaction.

But you know this is a test and tests are tricky. Your eye reads further down and you see "B" is a plausible answer, and then you are stopped in your tracks.

"C" means you have to tease out the BEST response, and this involves putting "B" on trial for its life.

If this answer isn't solid, you'll blow it by marking "C."

Clearly, your first impulse, to skate by using only your Fast thinking speed won't achieve an optimal result.

You must use Slow thinking, instead. Deliberately now, you go back to "A." Is this as solidly correct as I first thought? You ask yourself is there is a trick in the wording, a subtle shift that makes this appear perfectly correct, but it isn't.

Satisfied there is no trick, you confirm that "A" is correct. It must be included in your final answer.

Now, you turn to "B." Is this also true? Is there a trick in the wording?

You're convinced "B" is also a correct answer and thus "C" is the best overall answer inasmuch as it says BOTH "A" and "B" are correct.

If you overinvested in this question, and now you find you're running out of time, you may have to speed up your replies to the remaining questions. This is an enticement to use Fast thinking, again.

And Fast thinking will be fine with those questions where there isn't a "C" type of answer calling for Both of the prior questions to be true.

All you have to do with regular questions where ONLY one reply is true is to find it and mark the answer correct, or use the process of elimination and identify the ones that are clearly not true and select the one that seems least false.

The savviest test takers are not only good students of the underlying topics. They are great at deconstructing examinations while they are taking them, spotting tricks, and realizing when and where they need to REALLY slow down to not be fooled.

For example, I have a California Real Estate Broker license. Every four years it needs to be renewed and this calls for taking about 48 hours of coursework and passing several exams.

I just went through this process last week. What I like about the company I use for the training is that they offer quizzes that you can take and retake until you are confident and totally familiar with what will be asked on the exams. Correcting your errors on the quizzes, you learn what you missed and you reinforce what you got right.

But I have an advantage most test-takers do not have. I'm super test savvy.

As a lawyer, I have already prepared for and passed the most difficult multiple-guess exam in the universe, the California Bar Examination. I can take a real estate quiz and have a 50/50 chance of passing it without cracking a book, with no prior study, whatsoever.

This means I can score a 70, out of 100 available points.

Not bad, but if I score a 69 or less, I'm dead, and that is just as likely as my passing without any effort.

So, if my overall objective is to assure I'll pass, I need to do SOME studying, which requires some SLOW THINKING.

But here's what happens. I start studying and I enjoy what I'm learning. This makes me want to learn more.

I take quizzes and pass, but I don't pass with flying colors. I can do better, so I study harder, making a game out of tracking my improvement.

Exams are spaced over several days, and I'm chomping at the bit to take each one.

On some, I score a perfect 100%. On the rest, I score a fairly solid 86%. (Zipping too quickly through the latter, I actually skipped two questions, entirely.)

In any case, I have passed everything and I can renew my license.

What we need to guard against is being too cerebral or too impulsive. In other words, we should to use the best thinking for the occasion.

In the book, *Blink: The Power of Thinking Without Thinking,* author Malcolm Gladwell demonstrates how uncannily accurate our first impressions can be.

When we meet a person, we size them up in a few seconds. Through a process Gladwell calls "thin-slicing," we are able to gauge what is really important only from a narrow amount of experience.

He says our snap-judgments and decisions are often as accurate and sometimes even more accurate than our carefully planned and considered ones.

Experts typically fare better with their snap-judgments than amateurs.

One of my former consulting clients called me a few years after I had concluded a program with him. He had a product that he wanted to market primarily by telephone and he asked me if it could be done.

My impression, which came to me in about two seconds, was that this initiative would be a failure. The product was too technical, so describing it, getting people to feel confident enough about ordering it, sight-unseen, was asking too much.

I felt folks would need a demonstration and this would not be feasible with a single outbound call.

But I wasn't 100% confident about my reply and I wanted some time to consider my opinion, to test the contrary thesis, that it could be sold this way.

So, I withheld judgment and did not reveal my first impression. He decided not to pay me for a consulting day, and leaped ahead and invested millions in his marketing campaign.

He lost a ton of money.

My snap-judgment was right.

His, that he could do what he proposed, was not.

The moral to the story is if there is a lot riding on your decision, it pays to take some time to think your way through it and to weigh alternatives. Acknowledge your gut feelings, but when you can, confirm or disconfirm them though added thought, or better yet, through actual testing.

In the case of my client's gizmo, he could have easily compensated me for my quick thoughts or he could have paid me to do a pilot program where we actually tried to sell the device on a limited basis before rolling out a cost-intensive campaign.

Peter F. Drucker, management sage and my MBA professor, said: "There are risks we cannot take, and there are risks we cannot *NOT* take."

Distinguishing between them is essential to surviving and to prospering.

Most companies have to have an Internet presence, a web site, simply to be credible. People expect to learn about those with whom they are doing business.

But the amount of web presence is the risk-taking decision that must be made. Are you in a business that will be swallowed whole by competitors if you don't make radical adjustments in your business model?

The insurance industry has been one of the most traditional in the world. It has used brokers and agents, real people, sitting in real offices.

But now, you can buy insurance on the Internet though companies that have no local agents or brokers. If they are cheaper than traditional outlets, then it is only a matter of time before they gobble up the majority of policies.

Developing an Internet-only purchasing option is a risk carriers cannot afford to NOT take.

Fast thinking might say, "We don't want to go there," so we'll avoid pulling the trigger.

Slower thinking comes up with a different result. "People like the convenience and apparent economy of Internet shopping, so this is where customers are going. We have to get in front of the parade!"

This is not to say one needs to abandon the old ways. Our thinking needs to be nuanced enough to detect the subtleties.

Television was going to replace radio and movie theaters. It didn't.

Cable TV foretold the end of "free" TV. That didn't happen, either.

The Internet was going to replace brick and mortar shopping. It has gained an increasing share of the market, but malls and stores still exist.

So, we see that "either" one option or another isn't quite likely to occur.

We have to be on the lookout for "both" to be the accurate answer, for decisions and our best thinking to be both Fast & Slow, intuitive and deliberate.

Back to the client selling that device. The answer he really needed to hear wasn't a "Yes, it can be sold" or "No, it cannot be sold" by phone.

He really wanted to know, and should have been asking, "Can it be sold, PROFITABLY" though this medium.

If you do enough of practically anything, you'll get some results. I have said as much in my best-selling audio program, "The Law of Large Numbers: How to Make Success Inevitable."

In any large population there are a few early-adopters, folks that are the first on the block to try or to buy. They were first to have a hybrid or electric car in the driveway and solar panels on the roof.

You know the type. You may even be such a person.

These folks would have taken a chance on my client's new product, providing they were sufficient enthused and convinced of its modernity.

Could it be sold, by phone, to THEM?

Yes.

Could these trendsetting folks be culled into a list and be called first to introduce this fellow's new product?

Possibly.

So, there was a conditional yes I could have provided to my client's initial question, with a little thought.

Early buyers could have been farmed for testimonials that could be used to convince later buyers, those in the mainstream of adopters.

But note how nuanced these answers are.

This is what a combination of thought speeds can accomplish.

When you're emotionally aroused or provoked, the sage advice is to allow yourself 10 seconds to cool-off before responding.

This way you can benefit from both fast and slow thinking.

32

Choose Optimism:
Treat Bad News As Good News

Our quality of life is directly linked to whether we are optimists or pessimists.

There are some vital differences in pessimists, as studied at great length by University of Pennsylvania psychologist Martin P. Seligman.

Specifically, when negative events occur they are more likely than optimists to perceive them as (1) Permanent; (2) Pervasive and (3) Personal.

So, let's say you're a pessimist and you just lost your job.

Instantly, you'll be likely to conclude that you'll be unemployed for an extended period of time. Thus, your opinion of your success prospects will be dim, and you'll be less likely to jump back into the employment market than an optimist.

You'll do fewer of the essential things that will make you immediately employable because you'll believe it isn't possible to bounce back right away, so why bother?

You won't update or polish your resume. You'll look at fewer employment ads. You won't tap your network of friends and past associates for job leads.

You'll hesitate before interviewing, and when you do interview, you'll do it halfheartedly.

You'll interpret the rejections you get as permanent, too. Instead of following up after them with inquiries to the same companies, you'll toss the names and numbers of those contacts.

Let's say the reason for your termination was that your company is experiencing cutbacks because of reduced demand for its products or services. If you're a pessimist, you'll tell yourself, "Things are bad all over."

Because one company is in a rough spot, all companies are. There may be truth in the idea that we're in a recession or at a point in the economic cycle where employment is shrinking.

Tuning in the news, you'll pay particular attention to articles and statistics that support the idea that unemployment is pervasive.

And you might be inclined to perceive your lack of work as having something to do with you, personally.

"I'm just not cut out to be an employee," you may tell yourself. Or, "Bosses hate me," you could repeat to yourself.

By believing that your job status is permanent, pervasive, and personal, you pretty much make it impossible to be resilient and to find something else, especially right away.

Optimists are the opposite. In the extreme, they are somewhat like Pollyanna. There is a bright side to everything. They see the good news in the bad.

"They did me a favor," you could assure yourself, thinking that your future will look better than the past.

Believing that unemployment is temporary, you're likely to jump right back into the action. You'll update and polish that resume and send it out widely.

You'll find a list of the "Best Companies to Work For," and contact these firms.

You'll be likely to tap "The Hidden Job Market," which is finding those jobs that are open yet unadvertised to the public through the usual channels. How do you do this?

You identify the people in companies that you'll report to and contact them, directly. And you don't just email resumes. You follow up with phone calls, leaving voice mails to express your keen interest.

In other words you're likely to do all of the things that will make you stand out from the crowd of other job seekers.

I've done this very thing many times in my career, using multiple channels to reach out to influential people, including company presidents and CEO's. If you'd like more tips about career building in novel and lucrative ways, refer to my recent audio program, "How To Be Paid Far More Than You're Worth."

For our purpose here, you should note that optimists are doing more than perceiving the glass as half full.

They're taking action based on the idea that their lack of a job is temporary and not permanent.

You've heard people say that job hunting is a job in itself. This is exactly the way optimists look at the challenge. They aren't sidelined long because they don't equate unemployment with idleness.

They appreciate that they need to tackle the challenge of finding their next job in the same way they would jump on their next task at work, if they were working.

Optimists also see their problems as localized and not as pervasive.

If you're laid off from Company A, this fact has no bearing on the employment prospects at Company B. Yes, that industry may be in decline, but where one business fails, quite often, a winner steps up to manage the loser's abandoned accounts.

One firm weakens, but another strengthens.

But let's say an industry is in decline, what then? Leave it!

Search elsewhere. Especially if you're pessimistic and your default setting is to believe that employment grief is widespread, then you should look beyond an industry's confines.

Spread out and you'll prove that job woes are localized.

Finally, you need to believe that your unemployment is probably not about you, as an individual.

But let's say it is. If you rub people the wrong way and are always having conflicts at work, then, yes, something could be the matter.

Then, you should take a Dale Carnegie class or take an Extension class at a local college or university to polish your people skills.

It is said that the number one reason people succeed or fail in their careers is the extent to which they get along with and have a positive effect on others.

I've devised a cover letter that is to be used when sending out a resume. It says there are "Five Reasons You Should Hire Me."

Most of these reasons say that you get along with people and are a pleasure to work with.

This is a phenomenally effective letter resulting in a record number of interview invitations and ultimate job offers.

You want to appear to be the person who plays well with others in the sandbox.

But let's say you are an okay communicator and like most folks you don't have that many conflicts with others.

It could be a matter of office politics or group chemistry that led to your dismissal. It happens.

Manny Ramirez was a great hitter with the Boston Red Sox. But that team felt he was a pariah, and one pitcher even labeled Manny as a clubhouse "cancer."

The Red Sox were willing to trade Manny for nothing in return! They would pay the remainder of his huge salary to any team that would accept him.

Unpopularity doesn't get much worse than this.

Needing a good batter, the Los Angeles Dodgers decided to take a chance.

Instantly, Manny was a hit, in more ways that one. He hit numerous homeruns and extra base hits.

The fans loved him and he breathed life into the flagging Dodger season. Through his exertion and influence the team reached the postseason.

Center field, where Manny played, was painted with the word, MANNYWOOD, in his honor.

From hate to love, from exile to adoration, this was the path Manny's career took, practically in the blink of an eye.

What might have been his downfall in Boston, his outsize personality and emotional level of play, became strengths in Los Angeles.

So, was his failure in Boston "personal?" Not really, because the same personality thrived in a different town.

The same can be your fate by changing companies.

If you like where you are right now, if you're generally pleased with your life, looking back on the events that got you here, you'll probably see the necessity of them.

One thing led to another, and here we are.

There is a famous anonymous story about a farmer that illustrates this point.

Once upon a time, there was a farmer in the central region of China. He didn't have a lot of money and, instead of a tractor he used an old horse to plow his field.

One afternoon, while working in the field, the horse dropped dead. Everyone in the village said,

"Oh, what a horrible thing to happen." The farmer said simply, "We'll see." He was so at peace and so calm, that everyone in the village got together and, admiring his attitude, gave him a new horse as a gift.

Everyone's reaction now was, "What a lucky man." And the farmer said, "We'll see."

A couple days later, the new horse jumped a fence and ran away. Everyone in the village shook their heads and said, "What a poor fellow!"

The farmer smiled and said, "We'll see."

Eventually, the horse found his way home, and everyone again said, "What a fortunate man."

The farmer said, "We'll see."

Later in the year, the farmer's young boy went out riding on the horse and fell and broke his leg. Everyone in the village said, "What a shame for the poor boy."

The farmer said, "We'll see."

Two days later, the army came into the village to draft new recruits. When they saw that the farmer's son had a broken leg, they decided not to recruit him.

Everyone said, "What a fortunate young man."

The farmer smiled again—and said "We'll see."

Moral of the story: There's no use in overreacting to the events and circumstances of our everyday lives. Many times what looks like a setback, may actually be a gift in disguise. And when our hearts are in the right place, all events and circumstances are gifts that we can learn valuable lessons from.

*   *   *

Optimism and pessimism are really extreme states of mind. Inherently, they're distorted.

No one is a 100% pessimist. That dismal soul would never get out of bed or accomplish anything.

And there are events that can surely rattle the most ardent optimists, while other maladies can shake them to their foundations.

But we return to a theme that I mention again and again.

We can choose or at least modify our thoughts. Repeated thoughts create an outlook and a predisposition or a program for handling life.

It is more constructive to choose optimism because Seligman's research proves, and our everyday lives confirm the fact that optimistic people are happier.

Back to those Los Angeles Dodgers we go, for a moment. Manny and Mannywood came and went.

New owners and new managers were put into place. As I share these words with you, the team has come off of five consecutive Western Division championships.

Yet they lost in the postseason and they haven't won a World Series since 1988.

Do they have a chance to win it all? I'm not so sure, anymore. They've traded away one of the best pitchers in baseball. And they haven't replaced him with quality players.

So, I'm pessimistic about their possibilities.

And I'll probably be proven right. They won't have

the firepower to make it any farther than they have done for the past 30 years.

This ownership group with its billions of dollars to invest will cut back instead of taking the financial risks required of championship caliber teams.

They'll disappoint the fans, again and again.

But I hope I'm wrong. As a fan, I'd rather be wrong in my projections and see a winning team than be 100% correct and watch another losing effort over the course of many months.

They say pessimists are right more often than optimists. Optimists exaggerate the possibilities for success.

The odds are generally worse than they're willing to believe.

As pilot Han Solo barked in the original "Star Wars" movie, "Never tell me the odds!"

Don't confuse an optimist with the facts, is the joke.

But where does hope enter into the equation, what is referred to derisively as wishful thinking?

Pessimists dismiss hope. If it is a beam of light, they shut it off. It won't last, anyway, so why bother?

Farmers have to be the most hopeful people around. They plant seeds in the cold of winter and don't see anything for their efforts, over the chilly months.

Droughts can prevent the seedlings from sprouting. Pests can attack them when they do.

So many things can go wrong.

But this doesn't deter farmers from planting, and hoping.

The old adage may still apply when it comes to managing optimism: Hope for the best, but plan for the worst.

So, this year, I'll be watching the Dodgers with one eye.

The other one will be watching the Cubs!

33

Overcoming Fearful Thoughts

Fear is your friend . . . sometimes.

If you're pushed to the edge of a cliff and you peer down into an abyss, then fear is probably a good response, followed by removing yourself from the precipice.

When we're afraid, chemicals such as adrenalin are released into our bloodstream enabling us to flee or to fight.

This process helps a mom to suddenly summon superhuman strength to lift a car off of her trapped child.

There is survival value in being afraid, providing the object of fear is real and we act decisively to eliminate the source.

Once when I was walking down the steps behind my house adjacent to the Angeles National Forest, my wife warned me that there was a rattlesnake coiled two steps below.

I raised my right foot and stomped it to death.

You see, my downward momentum was such that I couldn't turn around and go up the steps. So, applying what I had mastered in karate, I eliminated the object of fear.

This is a dramatic example, to be sure. But the elements I mentioned were in place: (1) The object of fear was genuine, it was real; and (2) I acted decisively to eliminate it.

Few of our fears are like this one. Some say we are hard-wired through evolution to fear snakes. So it is very real, indeed.

Most of our fears are artificial. Take the fear of public speaking as an example.

I taught public speaking at the college level for five years, and I am a paid, professional speaker to this day. I address major conventions as well as corporate sales and customer service meetings.

I also teach at UCLA and U.C. Berkeley Extension on a regular basis.

So, what I'm going to tell you is pretty solid from an academic as well as a pragmatic standpoint.

The Book of Lists featured a survey that rated the fear of public speaking ahead of the fear of death!

Many people experience stage fright. The idea of having to give a talk, especially in front of strangers, is debilitating.

They get sweaty palms, their minds race, and they become noticeably jumpy.

All of these symptoms suggest that the fear they're experiencing is real.

But I'm here to tell you it isn't the same as fearing that rattlesnake. Compared to the risk I faced, standing on your hind legs and delivering a brief talk is a walk in the park or a balmy summer day at the beach.

The vital difference is that if you miss hitting the mark with an audience they'll be moderately disappointed. But miss hitting that snake in the right spot with the proper thrust and you could be bitten and die.

What we fear in front of an audience is embarrassment, shame, and a loss of face. Our egos are threatened.

Little more than vanity is at stake, typically, when we stride (or crawl) to the front of a public speaking class to deliver a talk.

I had to deliver a major talk at a university in the Midwest to win a job as a communication professor. They wanted to see how a teacher of public speaking could do when addressing a mixed group of students, colleagues and administrators.

A lot was riding on the success of that chat. For one thing, if I was hired that could turn in to a job for life because it offered the possibility of tenure some seven or eight years later.

Was I afraid; Not exactly. Long before that point I had learned to transform performance anxiety into a sense of excitement. Like alchemy, I would routinely take fear and transmute it into the gold of motivation.

That Indiana audience wasn't there on the basis of kill or be killed, as was the snake. They were going to be polite, no matter what.

They could decide not to offer me the job. But I wouldn't starve if that happened. I simply wouldn't teach there.

When facing a fear, we should ask that question which psychologists are fond of using when calming their overwrought patients:

What's the worst thing that can happen?

Typically, it is not so bad. It certainly isn't awful, though it may be mildly uncomfortable.

Most folks in advanced countries where survival isn't always threatened should go through what I will call, Rejection Training. In it, there would hear no after no. They would be told they're guppies in a world of sharks.

Deliberately, they'd be ridiculed and degraded, verbally.

And they'd learn to laugh in the face of it. They'd give as good as they got by returning every barb with one of their own.

You've heard that silly quip, "I laugh in the face of danger" that so many superheroes are fond of.

Well, to a point, I try to do that very thing. Sometimes I don't even have to try.

When I was training for my black belt in karate, which took an intensive eight years to earn, I'd get hit when sparring. On a few occasions, I'd react with a smile or with a laugh.

I wasn't masochistic. I prefer not to be hit. But I knew my opponent had lost control at the moment he or she made contact. Somewhere in my consciousness, that fact tickled me. Contact signaled victory.

It is well known that we can't dictate what is going to happen to us in life, but as a general rule, we can control how we react.

Something may scare us. But we don't have to permit it to disable us.

Let's go back to the public speaking example. Why are so many folks so afraid to talk before a group?

For one thing, they don't do it very often! Most of us are concerned about achieving in unusual situations.

There are organizations such as Toastmasters International that help people to grow comfortable when speaking in front of groups. They are exceedingly effective because they require members to get up at least once during every meeting to say something.

By dint of repeated exposures to what was the frightening trigger people experience huge transformations. Their confidence increases. Wallflowers become chatterboxes.

This is referred to as *systematic desensitization*. Repeatedly doing what you fear to do spells death for that fear.

Instead of dodging thrown tomatoes Toastmasters speakers are applauded. They're rewarded, not punished.

Psychologist Albert Ellis was ranked as one of the three most influential members of that profession. He developed a routine called Rational Emotive Behavior Therapy. I had the pleasure of studying with him at the University of California, Riverside.

His concept is based on the fact that most of our anxieties and fears are overblown. If we take a few seconds to dispute them we can overcome them.

Ellis was a sickly and shy child. By his own estimate, he was not a compelling physical specimen, and therefore wasn't inherently attractive to the opposite sex.

He had to work for attention.

He decided to purposely speak to 100 women at a botanical garden in his native New York. Initially, this was excruciating, because he was bashful and far from being a Lothario.

And his advances *were* rejected, one after the next. But instead of daunting him, he was emboldened.

He became outgoing. He asked some of the women out on dates.

His communication ability soared.

He found as long as he allowed his fear to get the better of him he was paralyzed. He had to overcome the thought that it was "awful" that he was about to face inevitable rejection.

By disputing the belief that something was awful he started to make it manageable.

"On what authority do I say this is awful? Will I be painfully skinned alive if I fail? Now that's awful, but practically anything short of physical torture is much less than awful."

He purposely changed the word "awful" to "mildly uncomfortable" in his mind. This enabled him to take action and to wade into the forbidding currents of rejection.

So, his thoughts used to say:

It's awful whenever I try to meet women, and I must avoid at all costs doing what's awful. Therefore I won't try to meet any women.

This became:

It's mildly uncomfortable whenever I try to meet women. I can get through mild discomfort, so I will try to meet women!

Some pundits say FEAR or F.E.A.R. stands for: False Evidence Appearing Real.

There is much wisdom in this, I think. Most of our fears have nothing to do with snakes or with life and death, imminent situations.

They are remote concerns, at best. The wolf isn't at the door, now. Typically, we have time to address and to remedy the sources of our concerns.

My advice to scared public speakers is to speak often and to prepare. If they are dreading a future engagement then I propose postponing their concern until the time arrives.

Tell yourself, "I'm not going to worry until ten minutes before I get up in front of the group."

Believe me. This works wonders. By rationing the amount of time you'll allow yourself to be concerned and by postponing it, you free up a lot of your attention and energy in the NOW.

Worrisome thoughts dissipate our energies. And the objects of our fears seldom actually come into being.

As a rule, I fight every traffic citation I receive. I'm an attorney and I realize there is always a defense one can summon, and it is up to the court to determine guilt, not me.

So, I set court dates, knowing there is a one-in-three chance the officer that cited me will not even show-up. That means the case will be thrown out and my driving record will remain clean.

This has happened more than once! In fact, my most recent speeding ticket was expunged in this manner.

(Just so you'll know, I'm driving at a safer rate of speed. I don't want to press my luck.)

Going to court, being sworn in, giving testimony, being examined by a judge or by an attorney, arouse fear in most folks. But what if you sincerely believed you would be proven not guilty or the case would be dismissed? You'd have a different attitude, correct?

So, why dread these things when you can choose to experience them as mildly uncomfortable, instead?

If the object of your concern is remote, such as a tax audit, or having a flood from a winter storm lash your home, you're a fool to waste time being in a state of fear or anxiety.

It is the very remoteness of the problem that should be a signal to you that your fear is exaggerated or is unwarranted.

Prepare your taxes correctly and purchase flood insurance, if you are that worried.

There is often an obvious fear and a hidden one.

Back to floods and taxes for a moment: We may be afraid we'll be victimized by these events. But the buried concern can be even more debilitating, that we'll be unable to handle the event should it occur.

This belief that we'll be inept in the face of a crisis is often worse than experiencing the crisis, itself.

Take this belief and do what Dr. Ellis would do: *Dispute it.*

Ask yourself, "What evidence do I have that this event will be cataclysmic and I won't be able to cope with it?"

Substitute, "It may be uncomfortable and it may be challenging, but I'll rise to the occasion."

Project confidence and competence into your future. Tell yourself, "Whatever comes along, I can handle it."

And what if you're wrong? What if you are less than perfectly competent and capable when something happens down the road?

Will you have been living a fiction?

If feeling buoyant and confident are fictions, then they are constructive and helpful fictions. They empower us instead of siphoning off our energy and distracting us from what we should be doing in the here and now.

One of my grandfathers was new to this country. He sired seven children. A well-meaning friend asked, "Al, aren't you concerned you won't be able to feed them all?"

To which Grandpa replied, "The Lord provides."

To sum up, most of our fears are not real, at least not as real as being inches away from a rattlesnake.

They are overblown, exaggerated, and we need to dispute them to put them into perspective. They aren't awful, but instead, mildly uncomfortable.

Sometimes, as is the case with public speaking, we can overcome our fears by deliberately doing that which we fear, over and over again.

Other problems, like speeding tickets can go away by themselves, if we challenge them. Others are so remote, occurring in a possible future way down the line, that we are well served to put them aside until the time they become immediate challenges.

Albert Ellis tells us we may not be able to eliminate all of our fears. But we can dispute them and react to them in a more positive and less damaging way.

After all, fears are often the products of beliefs, which are simply thoughts.

34

Lifting The Fog of Thought

Yesterday as I was driving to get my customary mid-afternoon coffee I noticed a beautiful melody on satellite radio.

"Beethoven?" I wondered. It was almost too pretty to be his, so I checked.

The text read, "Wolfgang Amadeus" before cutting off.

"Ah, Mozart, yes it is a sweet melody," I corrected myself.

And then I thought about Mozart's middle name, Amadeus. I recalled the movie bearing that title, co-starring F. Murray Abraham, whom I have seen recently in two TV shows.

And then, out of the blue, I questioned the name, *Amadeus*.

"Where does that come from?"

Without hesitating, I deconstructed it. In Latin, I think it means, more or less, "Love of God."

"No wonder this is mentioned so frequently when Mozart's name is uttered," I smiled.

That's a unique moniker.

What's significant about this stream of thought is that I find it takes a calm frame of mind to solve linguistic mysteries.

When I am feeling successful, at ease, and not stressed, my mind solves all sorts of riddles that I wasn't aware I was harboring.

They say sleeping peacefully is a sign of a clear conscience. Similarly, working out these word-wonders is a sign that my mind is functioning well.

It's very important to have some sort of gyroscope that signals when your mind is in balance or out of it.

Frequently, I find I can't buy the sort of mindset that will enable me to solve the simplest problems. I make no mental progress at all.

It's like spinning my wheels in a snowdrift.

Possibly, I'm preoccupied with an upcoming event. Or I'm in the middle of a negotiation that is taking longer to consummate than I am used to.

I might be feeling under the weather, when all I want to do is hide under the covers with a box of Kleenex within reach.

During these dreary days I'm better off leaving bad enough, alone.

If I try to think my way out of my mental state I'll simply add to my woes.

You know the feeling. There is a problem to be solved, but instead of having the wherewithal to come up with a strategy, like a rubber band, all you do is snap back to the problem.

And it hurts. You feel stupid and inept.

In a way, you are, because if you are in a lousy frame of mind it does you little good to try to push for results.

My Dad was invited to give a speech at a sales meeting because he was the top-earning account executive at the company. He wasn't in the mood, but he felt he had to do it, anyway.

So he rose to the podium and said:

"I'll gladly tell you the secret to my success. Do you see that clock on the wall? It's meaningless. I pay no attention to it. I don't set the alarm. I get up when I want and have a nice, big leisurely breakfast around 9:30 or 10. Then I may make a phone call or two and see a prospect in the afternoon. And if I don't feel like it, I don't do it, because if I don't feel good I'm not going to sell anybody anything, anyway. Thank you."

The group was shocked. Some applauded wildly, never having heard such a maverick's voice in a sales meeting. Managers were flummoxed and dumbfounded. Was this the type of message they wanted their disciplined troops to hear?

But Dad was definitely onto something significant, which I'm echoing here.

When you're in a lousy mood, and you aren't thinking clearly, don't perform brain surgery!

I do believe we can alter our thought processes, but it takes effort. If you can't summon that effort, then leave things as they are.

By itself, quite often, the fog of thought will lift.

Providing you don't worsen matters with perfectionism. If you carry the belief, "I MUST always be at my best!" then you're headed for disappointment.

First, of all, this isn't true. Few occupations require absolute perfection while permitting zero room for error.

Maybe brain surgery is one of them.

Second, who said you must be perfect? Did your parents impose this impossible standard upon you? Did your teachers do it?

Dad knew there is no such thing as a perfect salesperson. You cannot sell everyone, and sometimes, you can't even summon the gumption to sell yourself on performing the act of selling.

But what if you absolutely have to perform? No one else can fill in for you? You have laryngitis and can barely make comprehensible sounds yet you have to deliver an all-day seminar, one that cannot be rescheduled?

This happened to me in Braintree, Massachusetts. I had been doing talk after talk in city after city and my voice simply broke down. By the time I had reached Massachusetts, it was missing in action.

I gargled with salt water. The night before the event, I rested my voice. And I prayed I'd get through the next day.

I wasn't pleasant to listen to, but my audience was compassionate. Mercifully, they didn't ask too many questions!

I got by, and they actually gave me very generous speaking evaluations.

Sometimes, with supernatural assistance, we can muddle through.

When there is no other option we simply have to do what we have to do.

But that's an exceptional circumstance.

At the Oracle of Delphi's temple there was a sign that read, "Know yourself."

Possibly, this was the wisest thing pilgrims to that site would hear.

When it comes to thinking, whether you are doing it well or you are obstructed, you should heed these words.

Like taking your temperature when you're not feeling well, take the measure of your thoughts.

Are you problem solving easily? Or, are you obsessing over problems without talking a second to consider possible solutions?

Are you stuck on the same things?

What you may need to do is to deliberately interrupt your pattern. Change something.

Examine your personal routine. Are you eating the same stuff at the same time every day?

Substitute foods, or merely change the schedule.

Take a walk. Jog a few paces.

Stretch at your desk.

Slap water on your face.

All of these shortcuts can interrupt your patterns, dislodge stuck thinking, and lift the fog.

35

***

Give Up Resistant Thoughts

You WILL be hit!" my martial arts instructors repeated.

They wanted to set my expectations at a proper level. There's no such thing as sparring without mistakes happening.

Inevitably, even the most cautious practitioner will be kicked or punched if only by mistake. And we need to accept that this will happen, without shutting down.

Our survival may be hinged to our ability to keep fighting long after we've been hurt or have experienced pain.

In a fight, in other words, you can expect to encounter resistance.

But this expectation of friction needs to be moderated. You cannot or at least should not emit a vibration that says you expect a fight. That could cause hostilities.

As a martial artist you learn that avoiding a fight is the highest goal. If you can win without throwing a single strike or kick and without having to defend against someone else's flurry of moves, you have accomplished something very meaningful.

Many of us waste time and energy expecting bad outcomes. We expect flack and thereby cause it.

Let's say you need a raise in pay, and you're going to ask for one. What's the next thought you're likely to have?

You'll calculate the odds of getting your wish.

"Gee, she'll never say yes," you might tell yourself. Or, you could predict, "This won't be easy."

By thinking in this manner you set yourself up to fail. Moreover, how can you not project a lack of confidence if you're fostering this belief?

If you think you'll be resisted, you've already set up that force, if only in your mind. That expectation is suddenly likely to surface if only because you'll telegraph your expectation that it will.

What if you detect this problem before it fully manifests? Let's say you think, "This won't be easy," but then you hear yourself thinking it.

At that moment of perception, you have a choice. You can't retract that thought, removing it as if it never happened.

You know it happened.

But you can dispute it. You can bring in a second mind-voice. This one can ask, "Why expect resistance? Why tell myself it won't be easy?"

If you are feeling profoundly negative about your chances of getting that raise you can go on to ask: "What evidence do I have that this will be hard?"

If you haven't asked for a raise before, then you have no direct evidence that you'll be denied.

That will lead to a good insight. "If I have no experience asking for a raise on this job, or of my supervisor, then it may be likely that I'll get one."

That thought should cheer you up.

If the only evidence you have is second-hand because others have said management has turned them down, then you have to dispute the idea that their result will be yours.

Management may hold you in higher regard, or your supervisor may be in a good mood when you approach her with your request.

There is a famous story attributed to the ancient philosopher, Socrates. An excited fellow ran up to him and said, "You'll never guess what happened!"

"Before you tell me," Socrates said, "Let me ask you three questions."

"First, is this something you know personally to be true?"

"No," the fellow replied.

"All right then, is the news about someone you know, personally?"

"No, it isn't" he said.

"Is the news positive or negative?" Socrates asked.

"It's negative," the fellow conceded.

"So, you want to tell me about something you didn't experience and no one you know experienced, and it's bad news, as well? Say no more," Socrates grumbled, as he walked away.

Don't take on other people's negative expectations. Where they expect to encounter resistance, you may encounter none.

Plus, their assumptions about something could be built on sand, on mere speculation, and nothing more, as the Socrates story suggests.

When I was working on my Ph.D. smart people surrounded me.

But many of them doubted their intelligence and their ability to succeed. They would habitually recite horror stories.

There were tales about certain doctoral advisors that would flunk students on their qualifying exams, after two long and intense years of study.

Other stories were about students that passed their exams but then their advisors nit-picked their dissertations, requiring endless rewrites and elaborations.

This prolonged the time needed to finish the degree. Consequently, many students were in a scholastic Purgatory. Without the sheepskin, the doctorate, they couldn't advance their careers or qualify for the best teaching and research jobs.

They were stuck, and they had to take out costly student loans and it was a nightmare.

This sad outcome did occur every now and then. And it was also true that some advisors were more adversarial than others.

I found myself succumbing to the paranoia that these gossipers were purveying.

Realizing that I couldn't conscientiously do the work necessary to succeed while imagining such resistance, I deliberately challenged the veracity of what I was hearing and repeating to myself.

"What tells me I will be one of the victims?" I asked.

I was reasonably smart and I worked hard.

"If some professors are famous for frustrating their students' progress, is there a way I can avoid dealing with them?" I wondered.

I decided to ask one of my favorite doctoral professors with special training in psychology about his experience in his Ph.D. program, at the University of Washington.

"Were you as paranoid that you'd fail as so many of the doctoral students here seem to be?"

Calmly, he replied, "I figured they'd tell me one way or another if I wasn't cutting it, and if I didn't hear this I'd be okay."

My solution was interesting and it served me well.

I deliberately decided to believe the opposite of what I was hearing and to act accordingly.

First, I told myself, "My professors are going to HELP ME to succeed, and it is in their interest to do so. I'll be one of their shining successes, carrying on their legacy."

I stacked my dissertation committee with friendly, supportive faculty members who had a positive or at least a neutral reputation for awarding doctorates.

Then, I decided to act in a way that would assure their support. I started job hunting, applying for posts that required me to arrive with a doctorate in hand.

This meant they needed to write letters of recommendation, further cementing their positive perceptions of me.

While I was writing my dissertation I was a final candidate for a position in the Midwest. I got the job, finished and defended my dissertation, and my committee duly anointed me, "Dr. Gary!"

I changed the expectation from one of resistance to one of ease.

The question, as philosopher Ayn Rand put it, "Wasn't who will let me, but who will stop me?"

"No one," was the answer I told myself, and this turned out to be true.

I've seen something very similar in the workplace, especially among sales trainees.

If they build up this image that selling entails facing a mountain of resistance then resistance is what they'll elicit from their prospects and customers.

If you think it's hard then it will be hard.

Recently, I designed and delivered a sales training program for a seven year-old company. Headed by an entrepreneur who came to one of my public seminars, he thought sales were very hard to come by.

And his approach was to design presentations so they would address all kinds of resistance, in advance, before prospects raised any objections.

My method, to reduce it to its essentials, is to simplify.

"Take the straightest path to a yes," is my motto.

The presentation I designed for him did this and we trained some folks in my method.

But he wanted even faster results so he asked me if I would personally lead the way and make some sales.

I streamlined the approach even more and within the briefest time I closed the single largest and most profitable sale his company had ever earned.

It's true that I'm a sales expert and I have great methods many of which I have designed. But equally important is the fact that I expect selling to be easy!

I don't complicate it. My expectation-of-ease is something I communicate explicitly and implicitly to prospects. "Here's how it works" is one of the phrases I use.

I don't answer questions that aren't asked, and I don't rebut objections that are not made.

And it is common for my consulting clients to marvel at how quickly I am able to train and transform inexperienced salespeople.

I expect them to succeed, and I expect this to happen quickly.

I go so far as to say, if success doesn't happen right away I failed, or the person is wrong for that assignment.

Back to the martial arts we go.

One of the most important aspects of making a successful hand strike or kick is speed. Typically, the faster we are, the bigger the impact we'll make.

But there is an interesting problem novices have when they try to speed up. They slow down!

Here's how it happens.

Let's say a group of muscles, what we'll call "Group A" is required to execute the strike. By telling yourself, "I HAVE TO be faster" you flex an opposing set of muscles, "Group B," at the same time.

To move fast, Group B needs to be disengaged.

Here's how famous martial artist Bruce Lee explained the functioning of speed:

> "A powerful athlete is not a strong athlete, but one who can exert his strength quickly. Since power equals force times speed, if the athlete learns to make faster movements he increases his power, even though the contractile pulling strength of his muscles remains unchanged. Thus, a smaller man who can swing faster may hit as hard or as far as the heavier man who swings slowly."

He went on to make this essential, yet counterintuitive observation:

> "The less effort, the faster and more powerful you will be."

Give up your resistant thoughts. Replace them with images of ease and success.

36

How To Dash Self-Pity

Las Vegas was one of the last places I wanted to be.

I'm not lured to the gaming tables, but my audiences are.

When I've been booked as a professional speaker I've found it rattling when people stream in and out of a ballroom and pay more attention to the chips in their hands than the ideas I'm putting into their heads.

But there I was, the evening before I was about to deliver a talk before 300 people.

I was dreading it because I was doing it to promote my latest book, so the organization agreed to purchase hardcover books for all of its attendees if I would speak for no fee, except travel expenses.

Sorry, but I hate giving my stock in trade away. I'm a professional public speaker and I expect to make money when I keynote at a convention.

Hungry, having just checked-in the day before, with twilight at the horizon, I decided to trek to a nearby hotel to take advantage of its prime steak special.

Distances, like so many other things in Glitter Gulch, are illusory.

What looked like a few hundred yards was closer to a mile away.

When I arrived, there was a line for the underpriced dinner. Mostly there were couples being seated. As a single, I was off on the sidelines.

A weathered looking guy asked if I wanted to share a table so we could get served sooner.

"Sure, if you promise not to talk," I quipped, half-seriously. He agreed and we got a table.

He said he was an actor, there to shoot a prison picture with Wesley Snipes. I told him I had some acting background but I decided to get my performance jollies by developing content and delivering it through seminars and speeches.

He responded that the way he kept working was by writing screenplays that always featured a role for him. If studios wanted the scripts then they would often cast him as an actor, as well.

This was turning out to be a great conversation.

I confessed I was dreading my talk the next day, partly because I wasn't being paid.

He listened, closely and offered one word of advice.

"Act!" he said.

"Act?"

"Yeah, you know how to act, so act as if this is a great opportunity. When you take the stage pretend you're just where you want to be."

Wow, I thought. What a great piece of direction.

Of course, he was right. My attitude was totally wrong.

He was echoing something Dale Carnegie said about 70 years before:

"Act enthusiastic and you'll be enthusiastic. "

I knew this. One of my earliest college speech teachers was one of Dale Carnegie's first trainers. His entire career had been built on Carnegie's precepts.

I recalled how as students we would leap to our feet to speak at least once, every session.

Mr. Hayden was a sight with neatly clipped white hair, golf course ready outfits, and hearty smile. He was the embodiment of enthusiasm and a remarkable role model.

He had to be 70 years old, but he was in command. Not only was he a dynamo.

He was obviously successful.

His silver blue Cadillac was the flagship of the faculty parking lot.

Thirty years later, here I was, bereft of enthusiasm until that one-word tip turned me around.

My talk the next day was a big success. My book went on to be influential and it brought me, directly and indirectly close to a million dollars of speaking business.

I actually needed that Vegas audience to launch the book and to rekindle my enthusiasm.

Enthusiasm is the cure for self-pity. It is the functional opposite. You can't wallow and wail and be enthused at the same time.

At the base of self-pity is some kind of stinking thinking, undesirable thought.

In the Vegas situation, I was dragging this baggage with me:

1. Professionals are paid to speak. I wasn't being paid and so I wasn't being regarded or respected as a professional.

2. If you don't respect me, I don't respect me, either. And I don't respect you.

3. This is the basis of a lousy relationship, one that I shouldn't be in.

4. Free business at best leads to more free business, and I starve.

5. Free business is worse than no business, because I suffer costs.

6. In effect, I'm paying you so I can work for nothing. You're Tom Sawyer, getting me to whitewash Auntie's fence while convincing me to give you my stuff for the privilege.

7. I should never have said yes. I blame me.

8. Every minute until this gig is over is agony. I should be pitied for going through it.

9. If I'm not being paid I am stupid to give this gig my best effort.

10. You're audience will rue the day you didn't pay.

I don't like this train of thought. In fact, I hate even sharing it with you because it makes me seem peevish and small.

But it is the kind of destructive self-talk that leads to lose-lose relationships.

Looking at this thinking I have to say I'm really cutting off my nose to spite my face.

What good can come into my life from delivering a flat performance? If 300 people tell other people in the field that I am a so-so speaker, will that earn me any new gigs, ones that pay?

On top of this, why should I deny giving myself pleasure? I LIKE performing. Audiences, and especially larger ones, are fun and exciting.

I chose this profession in part because of the fireworks that go off when a great speaker meets his match, a great audience.

And here I was the night before a potentially gratifying event, where people had been primed to hear me, and I was miserable because of the thoughts I was thinking.

Who is this person? How far have I fallen from the tree of Carnegie and Hayden?

Self-pitying thoughts are exceedingly destructive because they rob us of our enthusiasm.

We like excitement, and we need good things to which we can look forward. Dragging ourselves to our tasks steals the possibility of joy.

And not only does it rob us. It also robs our "audiences," other people in our personal and professional lives.

The cure is so simple, as that actor reminded me.

Carnegie had more to offer than this one tip, power-ful as it is. He said we should find something positive in other people that we can appreciate, and show that ap-preciation by sincerely praising and complimenting them.

Likewise, I say we should find something positive in our situation, not only to stave off self-pity but also to embrace our possibilities.

That Vegas speech was, if nothing more, good prac-tice for me. I made a commitment and I was living up to it.

I sold hundreds of books for my publisher, showing good faith and living-up to my promise to help to pro-mote the title.

Plus, that event provided me with a good reference that I could pass along to others who would pay me to perform.

37

Eliminate Self-Criticism
& Stop Criticizing Others

Waking up this morning I started to recapitulate.

This is looking back at various episodes in your life for the purpose of liberating yourself from them.

The fact is most folks are tethered to the past and stuck in a black hole filled with emotions and bizarre thoughts. Much of our current effort is aimed at preventing ourselves from falling deeper into the darkness.

We don't want to repeat mistakes, but we feel powerless not to.

Recapitulating, deliberately remembering episodes from yesteryear can help us to become detached from their retrograde power.

I first encountered the concept of recapitulation when I read Carlos Castaneda, the anthropologist and novelist.

Anyway, today I was recapitulating intimate relationships, what I consider successful and unsuccessful ones. First, I noticed there are so many, it's amazing.

Quickly, I conjured up 50 key relationships with women. Then, I went on to teachers I've had in college and graduate schools. That's another 50 relationships, easily.

As I went from one to another, "breathing them out as Castaneda recommends" in an attempt to free myself from their gravity, I noticed something that is part of my stinking thinking.

I criticize myself, a lot!

My recapitulating was bogging down in thoughts such as, "This was stupid!" and "I really screwed-up, there."

It occurred to me as I was sipping my coffee gazing out at the boat docks and the canal that self-criticism is a huge waste of time and energy.

It isn't improving me. It is just making me feel lousy with guilt and second-guessing.

On some level I've bought into the old Socratic maxim, "An unexamined life is not worth living." Especially as a highly educated professional, a college professor with five earned degrees and thousands of students under my belt, I should be reflective.

At least, this is what I tell myself, a major premise from which I seem to have operated.

My actions should be deliberate and well reasoned. And a process of thinking is necessary if I want to become a more successful and happy person.

Self-criticism and self-improvement are tied together, in my mind. You can't get better I tell myself unless you label some of your actions as bad and others as good.

Now swigging my coffee in gulps of self-realization, I asked myself, "What if I simply swore-off of self-criticism? What if I put this behind me?"

Would life go on or would it come to a halt?

Musing over these questions something counter-intuitive occurred to me.

Is it possible that self-criticism, instead of leading to advancement is frustrating it?

Would I not only get more done but feel better about it if I showed every hint of self-criticism to the door and then went about my life undeterred?

Suddenly this cascade of insights showered down upon me.

Why do I worry so much? Isn't this just a pre-emptive form of self-criticism?

Procrastination-what's that about? We fear a bad outcome so we don't start? Isn't that just pre-emptive self-criticism?

This incessant judging of ourselves, I'm saying it simply has to go. The people that get on well in this world don't castigate themselves.

They're like pinballs. They crash into obstacles and bumpers yet each contact, no matter how repetitious or brutal, earns them points and oddly propels them forward.

Self-doubt, at least in academia, is thought to signify deep thinking. But those that cross the finish line seem to avoid it, or at least not be burdened by it.

Maybe they take a breather every now and then, but these are brief pit stops, where they gas-up, change tires in record time and burn rubber getting back in the race.

The concomitant of self-criticism is criticizing others. With few exceptions, this is another waste of mind-power.

If you're a parent, you're going to correct your kids. This is inevitable and necessary if you want to help them to survive and thrive.

Likewise, if you're paid to critique a beauty contest or to evaluate employees, then this is obviously rewarding. Everyone has to earn a living.

But it's all too easy, especially over the Internet, to waste gobs of time criticizing others.

This past year, alone, I've probably dropped 40 hours, a full working week at various blogs criticizing sports teams and their managements and politicians. Imagine that.

Even if I earned minimum wage for my exertions, that would be a car payment or four good tickets to the opera or ballet.

Worse, my comments have not led to constructive change. Surely, I haven't really influenced anyone except other goofballs that are wasting their time reading and reacting to my postings.

Especially, aided by technology, criticism of the type I've caught myself doing is habitual. It's way too easy to click on and return to blogs to see what others are saying and what they're saying or not saying about what I'm saying.

I'm not saying we should root out all diversions and forms of entertainment. It's just that so many act in an insidious way, ensnaring us in cycles that lead not only to distraction but also to experiencing raw and negative emotions.

So, what happens when we cease our criticisms of ourselves and of others? We create a vacuum.

We know nature abhors a vacuum. We're going to fill it with something. In my case, that's easy.

I have more books to write than I'll ever have time to address. And generally, I'm paid to write them, financially and emotionally they're gratifying.

So, there is really no contest between writing at blogs and wasting my time there, and doing what I'll take pride in that will provide benefits.

The *Tao Te Ching*, an ancient book of Chinese wisdom attributed to the sage, Lao Tzu, asks, "Can you wait for your mud to settle?"

This is the best thing to do when we create a vacuum, when we surrender limited or wasteful or even harmful thinking. Whether we're muckraking at blogs as I have done or we're criticizing our friends to other friends or griping about our families, when we desist, there is a whole lot of nothingness left over.

What do we do with it?

Let it settle, and "The right action will arise by itself," the *Tao Te Ching* advises.

From that point we can invoke the time tested wisdom of our parents and teachers, who often admonished: "If you can't say something nice, then say nothing at all."

Create silence in conversations, even in conversations with yourself.

Governor Jerry Brown of California, back in his Zen espousing days, said it this way: "Sometimes doing nothing is the highest form of action."

Which is sometimes translated by comedians as: "Don't just do something; stand there!"

And from that point what should we do? The key is to substitute better thinking.

Instead of criticism, what would that be? What form would it take?

As we'll see in so many cases of stinking thinking, the best antidote is to invoke the opposite kind of thought.

Instead of criticizing, we should praise.

This can be done by design.

We don't want to leave our thoughts or our words reverberating with a sour note. So, the tip is to tag onto a negative thought a positive one.

"I really screwed that up, but next time I'll do better!" is an example.

Let me give you a current example. Recently, I double-booked seminar dates with two different universities.

I had to be in two different cities 400 miles apart on May 7 and a week later on May 14.

Normally, this kind of snafu would mortify me. And when I realized what I had done, that was my first reflex, to castigate myself.

"How unprofessional!" I seethed. Immediately, I scanned my memory to reenact what I had done that led to this mistake.

I was tardy in buying a calendar for the forthcoming year, so it seems when I agreed to do the same dates at two sites I hadn't notated my commitments in the usual spots.

But, quite uncharacteristically, I went on to problem-solve. Dispassionately, I evaluated which of the two campuses would need to be sacrificed, if need be.

I was rolling out a new program at one school. I went through quite a gauntlet to get it approved. Plus, I was very interested in seeing how it fared in terms of its development, delivery and reception.

At the other school I was repeating a class that I do four times a year at that locale.

Plus, I was catching my error a full four months in advance of the upcoming double-booked program and I felt that school would be inclined to reschedule with me.

Even if we couldn't make the change, the school could still recommend the next scheduled session and carry over any registrations from the canceled class.

Immediately, I sent an email mentioning my error and requesting we bump the scheduled dates forward.

Almost immediately, I received a reply that read, "No problem. Which of these sets of dates do you prefer?"

The problem was solved with a minimum of fuss. Plus, I occupied that painful place of self-derision for a minimum amount of time.

As I look back on this episode, I find it very gratifying. A part of breaking the habit of self-criticism involves forgiving ourselves.

Right after labeling myself as unprofessional, I asked this objective question: "How many times have I screwed-up this way over the course of my career when scheduling university seminars?"

I have had an 18-year history at one of the schools, and a 10-year track record at the other.

I have also taught at 40 universities over the course of three decades.

NEVER have I double-booked!

Realizing this, a small voice in my head said, "I forgive myself!"

To err is human, correct?

Feeling poorly about yourself, which is the cause as well as the result of self-criticism, just isn't worth the effort or consequences. A down-in-the-mouth or dejected person isn't going to be of much good to anybody.

My action was negligent. I was not careful. I didn't dutifully log the dates of those competing programs.

Mea culpa.

But the best way to proceed is to avoid despairing, altogether. Try to be functional about shortcomings, mistakes, and mishaps.

Instead of wallowing in "Why me?" thinking, while answering, "Because I'm a bozo," we should be asking, "What's next?"

"Next," in the example provided, meant admitting the mistake as quickly as possible and engaging my university contact to adjust the dates. Yes, this was an inconvenience, calling upon him to do more administrative work. But every now and again, this sort of thing happens.

Why is there such a tendency toward self-criticism? I read somewhere that most high achievers in life are their own worst critics.

Doesn't self-criticism lead to improvement and to achieving even greater success?

If you want to be Mr. Universe, as actor Governor of California Arnold Schwarzenegger did, don't you have to relentlessly criticize your puny arms and legs? Don't you have to kick sand in your own face if you are a 98-pound weakling?

Especially in the absence of a coach or trainer barking at you, don't you have to at least growl at yourself?

Let me address this a few ways.

Perhaps as a spark plug or as a stick of kindling wood you need to get something going. Taking a hard look at yourself in the mirror can prompt you to start.

But at some point, if you want to develop and to sustain your gains you need to let go of any self-contempt you may foster.

Otherwise, it's too easy to fall into a funk, to think, "I'm not getting anywhere." Or you could tell yourself, "I'll never look good enough."

And then you'll quit, perhaps losing the gains you have achieved and ending up in worse shape than you we in when you got underway.

I'm not an expert in this area but I suspect this is at the bottom of most people's dieting failures. They start from a place of self-derision instead of self-love.

Instead of praising themselves as the pounds decrease, they criticize themselves because they still have too far to go.

Ironically, self-acceptance and weight loss may go together.

Instead of saying, "I hate this fatness" or "I must get skinny" because we are somehow humanly defective, we might do better to substitute these statements.

"I choose to weigh less" and "I no longer have a need for so much girth in my life" and "This heaviness isn't serving me well."

Self-criticism is a tree from which only poisoned fruit comes. If we start with self-negation, which is what criticism aimed at ourselves is, we'll always feel diminished by a sense of inadequacy and lack of fulfillment.

The fact that you are inclined toward self-criticism is actually a compliment to you. It means you are cognitively complex. You have an analytical mind. You're also eager to improve your lot in life. And you're taking responsibility for changing your life starting where change should begin—with yourself.

So cheer-up and recognize your strengths instead of criticizing your weaknesses.

I hope you've come to see in this program many of the thoughts that are helping you as well as indentifying those that might be holding you back.

I also hope you'll return to this program many times over when you feel stuck and you don't know why.

I'm sure you'll find as I have that the surest cure for stinkin' thinkin' is more and better thinking!

May your thoughts be happy and productive!

Good luck.

Index